AF229597

KALE YEAH!
IT'S STILL GOOD
NO MEAT NECESSARY
(Volume 2)

Brenda T. Bradley, PhD

Pearly Gates Publishing LLC
INSPIRING CHRISTIAN AUTHORS TO BE AUTHORS
Pearly Gates Publishing LLC, Houston, Texas (USA)

Brenda T. Bradley, PhD

Kale Yeah! It's Still Good – No Meat Necessary
(Volume 2)

ISBN 13: 978-1-947445-67-3

For information and bulk ordering, contact:
Pearly Gates Publishing, LLC
Angela Edwards, CEO
P.O. Box 62287
Houston, TX 77205
BestSeller@PearlyGatesPublishing.com

Disclaimers

All material in the *Kale Yeah! It's Still Good – No Meat Necessary (Volume 2) Cookbook* is provided for informational purposes only and should not be construed as medical advice or instruction. No action or inaction should be taken based exclusively on the contents of the information provided. Readers should first consult health professionals on any matter relating to their health and wellbeing.

In using this cookbook, you agree to hold Brenda T. Bradley, PhD, Pearly Gates Publishing, LLC, its owners, agents, and employees harmless from any and all liability for all claims for damages due to injuries (i.e., allergic reactions), including attorney fees and costs incurred by you or caused to third parties by you.

Testimonials have been submitted by users of the *Kale Yeah! It's Good – No Meat Necessary Cookbook* and "The 21-Day Vegan Challenge" ™. Each has a unique experience, eating habit, and applied the information provided in different ways. Thus, the experiences shared may not reflect your personal experience. Their testimonies are not intended to represent or guarantee that anyone will achieve the exact same or similar results.

Brenda T. Bradley, PhD

Food Handling

Please practice caution and proper sanitary practices when handling food products. Wash your hands and food surfaces thoroughly before and after handling any food product. Refer to the Health Department's "Safe Food Handling Guidelines" (www.fsis.usda.gov). Use your best judgment and proper discretion when preparing or consuming any food.

Testimonies and Applause for
Brenda "The Fairy Godmother of Food" Bradley, PhD

"It is with great joy that this testimony comes with heartfelt thanks. I've been overjoyed of how connecting with Dr. Bradley over the past few years has given me the motivation not only to eat but even stay more positive about what I choose to eat. It's helped me to identify not only what's better for my body, but even those in my family who will listen. Thanks, Dr. Bradley, for the connection and, most importantly, being a great witness to God's people."
~ **Norman Ray** ~

****

"In the old days, my plate, refrigerator, and cabinets were filled with unhealthy choices. Since I started following the guidance of Dr. Bradley, I pay more attention to food labels, make wholesome choices, and have noticed nothing but positive changes in my overall health. I look forward to diving into her next cookbook as I continue this exciting life-changing journey!"
~ **Terrace** ~
Richmond, VA

****

"Through it all, it's actually been fun trying new things such as "Buffalo Cauliflower Wings." Tasting these strange plants that actually taste like meat (jackfruit) and making sure my flours, rice, and pasta are any other color than white has been enlightening. Who knew I would be here — but I am and glad to be! Thanks, Dr. Brenda Bradley!"
~ **K. Armstrong** ~

"I was eating a healthy vegetarian diet for 20+ years. When I met Dr. Brenda Bradley, I learned how to easily transition to a plant-based lifestyle. Using her first cookbook empowered me to prepare healthy, delicious foods that are packed with great nutrition. Now, I enjoy spending time in the kitchen cooking – not to mention I have more energy for my workouts and enjoying life! Thanks, Dr. Bradley!"
~ Dr. Gerald Hassell ~
Clinical Psychologist

****

"It has been such an honor to work with Coach Brenda Bradley! This experience has really changed and blessed my life. My body feels so much lighter and more energetic! I really appreciate how awesome the meals taste because I can actually enjoy my food and am learning how to make easy substitutions. I am grateful for her commitment to this mission. I did not know so many [vegan] recipes were out there! Thank you for walking us through this, Dr. Brenda Bradley!"
~ Tierra Destiny Reed ~
CEO

****

"I've learned that I can live without meat. I feel and sleep much better. My energy level and endurance have improved. I have learned to make better choices when it comes to nutrition, and I can prepare healthy meals at home without having to settle for pre-packaged frozen ones. Thanks, Dr. Bradley!"
~ M. Rolfe ~

"Some people think eating everything that's fried in fat is okay. Kale Yeah: It's Good is an understatement for this amazing cookbook! It contains easy-to-follow recipes and can turn the most kitchen-challenged individual into an adequate vegan chef. Beyond boiling water, Dr. Bradley shows you how to turn healthy vegetables and fruits into delicious meals. This isn't "rabbit food," folks — and this book won't cost you a pretty "penne"!"

~ Ebony Chante' ~
Owner, Revolutionary Wellness
www.revolutionarywellnessatl.com

****

"Many years of eating what was put in front of me and not what was good for me led me to high blood pressure, elevated cholesterol levels, and borderline diabetes. Food as my medicine changed my mental, spiritual, and physical outlook. Dr. Bradley, thank you for your efforts, fortitude, and determination to make what we eat taste great as well as being good for us. Plant-based eating and cooking is fun, delicious, and enjoyable."

~ Lenister Brown ~

****

"Dr. Bradley, WOW! Your cookbook recipes are delectable, flavorful, and easy to follow. I can tell each recipe was created with love. I look forward to preparing every meal in this book!"

~ Molakai Teague ~
Washington, DC
Traci Lynn Jewelry
www.tracilynnjewelry.com/Molakai

"What started as JUST a 21-Day Vegan Challenge (with an emphasis on 'Challenge') in October 2016, is evolving into a journey of healthy lifestyle changes which are spiritually, emotionally, and physically rewarding. I describe my journey as slow-paced and very personal as I continue to make small changes in my daily walk. I do this by increasing the amount of plant-based foods in my diet, along with a consistent fitness program. Dr. Brenda Bradley and her "Helping Other People Evolve [H.O.P.E.] Support Group" have been instrumental by providing helpful information, group support, and encouragement to help me live my best life. I am a walking testimony to the positive benefits of plant-based eating."

~ Paulette Anderson ~
MEDCOM Ombudsman
Lawton, OK

****

"Kale Yeah: It's Good – Volume 1 is one of my staple cookbooks because the recipes are both easy and delectable. My all-time favorite is "NOT from the Sea Tuna." We use it with all of our cooking demos, and they sell out every time! I can't wait to get my hands on Kale Yeah: It's Still Good – Volume 2 because I know Dr. Bradley will overdeliver as usual."

~ Shadonne Harris ~
Owner, Balanced Body Massage Group
www.balancedbodymassagegroup.com

"I participated in Dr. Brenda Bradley's 21-Day Vegan Challenge in 2016. Her first cookbook, Kale Yeah: It's Good – No Meat Necessary, was a part of the challenge package and became an intricate part of my transition to plant-based cooking. For those just starting their plant-based journey, cooking can be a challenge all by itself, so Dr. Bradley provided pictures of the ingredients to give you an idea of what to pick up at the store. To date, I have perfected a few of the meals and have even made some of them with my adult children.

"The real conversation of how food can be used as our medicine became a topic of discussion with my children, as their interests were sparked on if the meals were flavorful. I have made over a dozen recipes from Dr. Bradley's cookbook, and my children agree that they are, indeed, delicious. A few of the meals I have made are: NOT from the Sea Tuna, Curry Chick 'n Dish, Vegan Eggplant Casserole, and I cannot forget her scrumptious No-Bake Apple Pie!

"I follow Dr. Bradley on social media, where she is also known as the "Fairy Godmother of Vegan Food." She has done an excellent job with the step-by-step instructions for her mouth-watering recipes. I always look forward to the new, delectable meals she shares, and I am never afraid to give them a try because they all have turned out scrumptious.

"Her plant-based recipes are not only used as medicine to give us the nutrients we need, but the love and joy by which she shares her recipes are good for the soul."
~ Rosemary Hill ~
Best-Selling Author, *The Other Side of Through*
Contracting Deputy Officer

Dedication

This cookbook is dedicated to my first love, my dad,
James Willie Dee Bradley, Sr.
Although he's not physically here,
he lives in my heart.

Rest in Peace and Love.
Your Baby Girl, Brenda

Acknowledgements

First and foremost, I will always give praise and honor to **God** for blessing me with the ability and strength to stay the course and accomplish such goals.

I am so thankful for my **Mom**, who asks and encourages me to send her recipes on a daily basis.

A very special thanks to my recipe "tasters," **Jarvis** and **Gerald**, for their honesty on whether the recipes were a *"GO!"* or a *"NO!"*

To **Retired Major Tamara McCutcheon** (Almost a Vegan), I salute your enthusiasm and willingness to jump in at a moment's notice to write such an awesome Foreword for this book.

To my motivator and business coach (aka my daughter) **Ebony**: Thank you for the conversations, laughter, and guidance that you are always willing to give.

To my son, **Brandon**: You went vegan for over 60 days and did such a great job! I'm looking forward to you preparing me a vegan meal!

For those who have joined **The 21-Day Vegan Challenge**, I extend this sincere *"Thank you!"* for your ongoing support, encouragement, and love. You really help me to stay focused.

To **Terri Taylor**: Even though she didn't do anything, she *IS* my best friend, and I give thanks for her devoted friendship. Oh, wait! Although she is not a vegan, she enjoys eating my vegan food!

And lastly, but surely not least, for those of you who have purchased *this* cookbook: I extend a heartfelt **"THANK YOU!"**

Foreword

When asked to write the Foreword for *Kale Yeah: It's Still Good – No Meat Necessary (Volume 2)*, I was elated and humbled. Dr. Brenda Bradley is a beacon of light for anyone looking to take charge of their nutritional health…*especially* those interested in a plant-based diet.

In my personal journey to eat healthier, I've participated in her **21-Day Vegan Challenge** *twice* and continue to use the program. I also had the pleasure of being a co-author in her 2017 book release, *I Feel Good: Real Life Testimonies from People Who Used Food as Medicine*. Dr. Bradley has made it her life's work to guide, mentor, and support healthy lifestyle choices—starting in the kitchen. I'm constantly inspired and challenged by her example and am truly blessed to call her a **friend**.

Dr. Bradley credits the turning point in her lifestyle change to switching from the Standard American Diet (SAD) to a plant-based diet. Her passion for living a plant-based lifestyle emanates through her Instagram page. If you aren't already, I implore you to follow 'docbrad67' (also known as "The Fairy Godmother of Food"). Her delectable vegan dishes come alive through video clips, photos, and nutritional/cooking tips. The Fairy Godmother of Food's expertise as a vegan chef is all the persuasion necessary to know the Kale Yeah cookbook series is a **MUST** for your kitchen and quest to healthier eating.

My favorites from her first cookbook release are: Blueberry Walnut Pancakes, Eggplant Casserole, and Vegan

Apple Pie. I'm excited to see what's in store next! All recipes are simple to follow and *beyond* delicious!

It's no surprise that Dr. Bradley is a leading Speaker and Expert in the vegan community. All are fortunate this multi-faceted Certified Integrative Nutrition Health Coach sees fit to share her heart and soul through a cookbook series. Her list of accomplishments speaks volumes, her passion for healthy living speaks louder, and her desire to help others pursue healthy lifestyles can be found in her vegan dishes.

Kale Yeah! It's Still Good – No Meat Necessary (Volume 2) will give you a **great** foundation for significant lifestyle changes. Enjoy your journey to healthier eating!

~ Tamara McCutcheon, USAF Retired ~
Chief Creative Officer, RETIRED CHICKs, LLC
www.facebook.com/RETIREDCHICKs

Introduction

I was born and raised in Arkansas and had a decent childhood. As long as the chores were done and schoolwork completed, we were allowed to play with friends in the neighborhood until mom called us home to eat.

My family **LOVED** to eat. We ate everything from fried chicken to smothered pork chops for dinner, and mama's fried apple pies and banana pudding for dessert. My mother was **THE BEST** cook on the block! She could turn a bag of flour and an egg into the most delicious cakes, biscuits, and pancakes ever!

I loved eating together as a family. Some of my fondest memories revolved around the dinner table in the beckoning warmth of love and, of course, the aroma from the kitchen.

My mother was very particular about the food we ate. She was a firm believer in eating breakfast, lunch, and dinner. She would often say, *"Growing children need to eat nourishing food."* Although I was eating "nourishing" food, I would become very sick and miss an entire week of school each year. The doctors were always puzzled because they would run several tests and could never figure out why I couldn't keep any food down and become dehydrated.

During the Summer of 1984, my brother, Jeff, who was in college at the time, came home for a visit. I loved when he would visit. He would share so many interesting stories about college life and the things he was learning. During this particular visit home, he told me that he had decided to stop eating animals and had become a vegan.

I had never heard of such a thing and began to wonder if Jeff was okay. *Had he joined some sort of cult that was planning to rise up and start rebelling against those of us who **were** still eating animals?* I looked up to my brother and admired him, but there was absolutely **NO WAY** I would *EVER* stop eating meat!

Jeff went on to tell me that eating animals would be the death of many people. I didn't believe him because our great-grandmother, Mary, was still alive—walking, talking, making us bologna sandwiches, cussing us out, and telling us how ***"God don't like ugly!"***

In 1986, I decided to join the United States Air Force. My first duty station was in England. I was so excited…and scared. This was my first time traveling out of the country. My parents and siblings were shocked but excited for me, too. I remember my mom and dad telling me that I better not get kicked out of the service and have to come back home to live with them.

I arrived at the Royal Air Force Lakenheath, England in November 1986. By January, I had become acclimated to the new locations and was enjoying the military. As March approached, I began to become very nervous. March was the month I would become very sick and unable to eat and walk. I didn't want to get kicked out of the military; therefore, I scheduled a doctor's appointment. During the appointment, I told the doctor about my past situation of getting sick and not able to attend school. After the doctor's examination, she recommended that I stop eating red meat.

I followed the doctor's advice. Well, March came and went—and I didn't get sick! I called my parents to share the good news.

I enjoyed being in the military and took advantage of the available opportunities. I was able to complete several college degrees and traveled around the world. After leaving the military, I was well-equipped to enter the corporate arena and made significant strides up the corporate ladder. I was so focused on making it to the top that I neglected taking care of myself. I was no longer fit and fabulous. I had gained over 75 pounds and struggled with high blood pressure, high cholesterol, depression, and prediabetes.

I knew I needed to lose weight, but regardless of my efforts, I kept losing the war against obesity. I was literally at my wit's end, and depression was beginning to take over my every thought of doing harm to self. I was miserable, and no one knew my pain and struggle.

One Sunday, I gathered enough strength to pull myself out of bed to attend church service. During service, the minister spoke about Lent, which is a traditional time for fasting or giving up something for 40 days. I wanted to participate but couldn't think of anything that I was willing to give up.

Then, it hit me!

I remembered my brother, Jeff, and decided to stop eating meat for 40 days...*ONLY!*

After 40 days, I had lost 33 pounds! As tears of joy ran down my face, I wanted to climb the tallest mountain to announce my victory!

The very next day, I treated myself to one of those fine-dining restaurants. I couldn't **WAIT** to devour my selection of fish. As soon as I took one small bite, I felt dizzy and became sick to my stomach. On the way home, I thought of suing the restaurant for food poisoning.

The following week, while at the bowling alley with my son, Brandon, I grabbed one of his French fries—and immediately felt dizzy and became sick. We left and headed home. On the way home, I began to worry. I didn't understand what was happening. ***Why was I getting sick?***

I soon learned from my younger brother, Jarvis, that my body had totally given up meat. I was turning into one of those "vegan people." I immediately thought about my other brother, Jeff, who first told me to stop eating meat in the early 80s.

As I continued to eat meatless foods, I was amazed at my weight loss and, within months, was taken off all medications because I no longer struggled with high blood pressure, high cholesterol, depression, obesity, and prediabetes.

Some of the healthy benefits noticed were:

➢ Weight Loss
➢ More Energy
➢ No "Brain Fog"
➢ Better Skin

There was **NO** way I would go back to eating meat, but I was clueless and confused. Determined to continue this lifestyle, I started doing research and would often attend vegan festivals and cooking classes. I became very intrigued with learning more about food and soon started whipping up meals at home. Thus, my first cookbook, *Kale Yeah: It's Good – No Meat Necessary*, was released in 2016.

Following the release of that cookbook, I also rolled out my program called "The 21-Day Vegan Challenge." It's a program that has been designed for **anyone** desiring to make a lifestyle change or to explore and experience the health benefits of a vegan or plant-based diet. I host the program monthly.

Living a plant-based lifestyle is a never-ending school of learning. I have and still am learning much about this lifestyle—especially the food. Not only does it excite me, but my family gets a kick out of how I'm able to turn fruits and vegetables into a healthy, delicious dish or meal…thus, giving me the name, "The Fairy Godmother of Food."

It is now 2019. For the past year, I have been in the kitchen turning flour into cinnamon rolls; mushrooms into seafood-tasting sandwiches; and jackfruit into meatless chicken and dumplings. My family has given me the green light, and it brings me much joy to introduce you to *Kale Yeah: It's Still Good – No Meat Necessary, Volume 2!*

From my heart to your table, **ENJOY!**

~ Dr. Brenda Bradley ~

Table of Contents

Ideal Pantry Ingredients and Kitchen Essentials

There are several misconceptions surrounding a plant-based lifestyle and thousands of questions, too. When I first "seriously" decided to make the lifestyle change, I often wondered and worried if I had set myself up for failure because there wouldn't be much to eat—and I **NEEDED** to eat! I was pleasantly surprised to find out there are a lot of dairy and meat-free foods, along with numerous ways to prepare fruits, vegetables, grains, etc. to create delicious meals.

Learning to prepare healthier food isn't hard, but I must admit it may be different than what you've known in the past. The ingredients and kitchen essentials may be new and may seem a little intimidating in the beginning. They were for me, too. However, it won't be long before you'll be smiling and zipping through the kitchen with ease. There are lots of plant-based ingredients. I will cover just a few broad categories to give you some examples to help you get started with stocking your pantry.

Herbs

Whether fresh or dried, herbs are fragrant plants whose leaves are used to add flavor to dishes. Some herbs to keep handy and available in the kitchen include:

- **Basil** (aromatic green leaf) – Used in pasta dishes, salads, marinades
- **Bay Leaf** (oblong leaf with a pungent aroma) – Used in stocks, sauces, soups, stews
- **Chives** (fine, green top of a small onion) – Used in salads, baked potatoes, soups, sauces
- **Cilantro** (light green aromatic leaf) – Used in salads, salsa, sauces, soups, dressings
- **Dill** (very pungent) – Used in salads, soups, vegetable sauces
- **Marjoram** (green herb from the mint family) – Used in stews, soups, vegetables, sauces
- **Mint** (an aromatic herb with cool flavor) – Used in fruits, teas, fruit beverages, peas, jellies
- **Oregano** (strong, pungent herb) – Used in Mexican and Italian dishes, tomato sauce, soups
- **Parsley** (green leaf; sweet flavor) – Used in stews, vegetables, potatoes, salads, garnish
- **Rosemary** (green leaf; resembles pine needles) – Used in sauces, soups, marinades, stews
- **Thyme** (small, brownish-green leaf) – Used in soups, stocks, salad dressing

Spices

Spices are derived from plant seeds and technically can be considered "plant-based friendly." Just make sure to check the label because some animal products do find or sneak their way into the spice blends, especially if produced in a commercially based factory. Some spices you may consider stocking include:

> - **Allspice** (small brown berry) – Used in cooked fruits, puddings, pies
> - **Cayenne** (hot red pepper) – Used in soups, sauces
> - **Chili Powder** (can be mild or hot) – Used in chilis, stews, sauces
> - **Cinnamon** (aromatic bark from a tree) – Used in bread, pastries, desserts, hot beverages
> - **Clove** (dried flower bud) – Used in stocks, sauces, fruits, cakes
> - **Cumin** (small seed) – Used in chilis, curry blends, salsas, vegetables, rice
> - **Curry** (a blend of spices) – Used in curry dishes, vegetables, soups, sauces, rice
> - **Garlic Powder** (dried bulb) – Widely used
> - **Nutmeg** (kernels of nutmeg fruit) – Used in baked goods, pies, bread, soups
> - **Paprika** (sweet red pepper) – Used in salads, sauces, dressings, garnish
> - **Turmeric** (the yellow root of the ginger family) – Used in curry powder, salads, stews, soups

Cooking Oils

When it comes to cooking oils, plant-based oils are better and healthier than most animal fats. Most oils are derived from plant sources, which means there are a lot of different oils from which to choose. Depending on the intended use, some oils work better for high-heat cooking (ranges from 225 to 510 degrees Fahrenheit), while others are better for low-temperature cooking, baking, or salad dressing. It's important to understand your options and choose accordingly.

For example, cooking with heat-sensitive oils can cause rancidity and oxidation (inflammation to the cells and free-radicals in the body). Therefore, it's best to look for organic, non-GMO oils and avoid "partially-hydrogenated" (trans) fats. Cold-pressed oils are typically healthier.

There are several healthy oils to choose from; however, I'm listing the top three (3) healthy oils I normally use:

➢ **Avocado Oil**
   To be honest, avocado oil is not cheap, but it performs quite well because it has a high smoke point of 520 degrees Fahrenheit. This oil is extracted from the fruit of the avocado tree. It is good for high-heat cooking and frying and can also be used cold in dips or recipes.

➢ **Extra Virgin Olive Oil**
   Extra virgin olive oil comes from olives. "Extra virgin" means it's unrefined and in a natural state. This oil has a smoke point of 375 degrees Fahrenheit and may not be

the best choice for high-heat cooking. It's great for sautéing vegetables at low heat and is often used as dressing for salads.

> **Organic Grapeseed Oil**
Organic grapeseed oil comes from grapes. It has a smoke point of 390 to 420 degrees Fahrenheit. You can use this oil for sautéing and high-heat cooking. It also works well with other recipes. Make sure to choose cold-pressed or expeller-pressed because other options may involve chemical processing.

A Few Staple Ingredients

Following is a list of a few staple ingredients you are most likely to find in my kitchen. Always be mindful that the quality of your finished product is related to the quality of ingredients you use. I encourage you to be selective and make sure you're choosing the healthiest products.

- ➢ **Agave Nectar** is an all-natural liquid sweetener created from the extract of the agave plant. However, I suggest when buying agave nectar, be aware of the type you are purchasing. Many brands sold claim to be "organic" but are nothing more than refined fructose.

- ➢ **Almond Milk** is a creamy beverage made from almonds. It doesn't contain cholesterol or lactose because it doesn't come from an animal. It has a rich, creamy texture and is a substitute for cow's milk.

- ➢ **Nutritional Yeast** (although the name is not appealing), also known as "nooch," is an inactive yeast. It's yellow in color and comes in flakes. It's often used as a condiment due to the savory, nutty, and cheesy flavor. In addition to the flavor, it's well-known for its nutritional value.

- ➢ **Chickpeas**, also known as garbanzo beans, are versatile and used in many recipes. They also come with a range of health benefits and are a good source of protein, carbohydrates, and fiber.

- ➢ **Spelt Flour** is a high-energy grain that is more easily digested than most other grains because of its high-water solubility. It has more protein, fiber, fat, iron, zinc, copper, and B-vitamins than wheat. It's great for making pancakes and bread.

➢ **Bragg Liquid Aminos** is a liquid protein concentrate that's gluten-free and made from non-GMO soybeans and purified water. It's a great alternative for soy sauce.

➢ **Earth Balance Butter** is a plant-based butter that is dairy-free, gluten-free, non-GMO, certified Kosher, non-hydrogenated, and is made with an expeller-pressed natural oil blend, which consists of soybean, palm fruit, canola, and olive.

➢ **Vital Wheat Gluten** is a type of flour that is all gluten with very little starch. It's considered a natural protein found in wheat. Although it can be used to make bread lighter, fluffier, and rise higher, I normally use vital wheat gluten to make a meat-substitute item.

➢ **Brown Rice** is a whole grain, meaning it contains the outer, fiber-filled layer called 'the bran,' the nutrient-rich core called 'the germ,' and the starchy middle layer called 'the endosperm.' This rice is low in calories, high in fiber, gluten-free, and can be incorporated into a variety of dishes.

➢ **Vegenaise** is a vegan mayo that is gluten-free, dairy-free, egg-free, and non-GMO. It can be used as a substitute for mayonnaise. There are soy-free substitutes as well.

Tools

Having the proper kitchen gadgets are quite beneficial for creating and preparing delicious meals, juices, and smoothies. Adding the following gadgets will help improve your culinary skills in no time:

> **Food Processor** – A food processor cuts your food preparation time considerably. If you don't want to spend a lot of time chopping vegetables, a food processor is very essential and makes chopping vegetables and preparing dough easier.

> **A Good Juicer** – Extracting juice from fruits and vegetables can be the most nutritious component to a healthy plant-based diet. You can feed all your cells and will save most of the energy your body uses to separate the juices from the solids. There are three (3) types of juicers, with the choice ultimately being yours:
> - *Centrifugal Juicer:* This type of juicer grinds the vegetables and fruits and pushes them through a straining basket at high speed, which can cause oxidation and rapid loss of nutrients. If using this type, it's recommended to consume the juice immediately.
> - *Masticating Juicer:* This is considered a "champion juicer." It crushes the fruits and vegetables after they pass through the chute and then separates the pulp and the juice by slowly squeezing the produce. The juice runs through a mesh, while the pulp is pushed through a

separate container. This juicer is multifunctional and can also work as a food processor or grinder.

- o ***Triturating Juicer:*** Also known as a "twin-gear juicer," this juicer basically has two gears that are assembled closely to each other. The gears rotate to crush and grind produce into very small particles and extract the juice by pushing out the dry pulp. As a result, the juice is nutrition dense and can stay refrigerated longer.

➢ **A Blender** – Blenders have many uses in the kitchen to include making smoothies to salad dressings and so much more. Purchasing an inexpensive blender will do a reasonable job, but eventually, it might be a better idea to consider a VitaMix. A VitaMix is a powerful machine that literally breaks apart the cell walls of foods, making digestion much more efficient.

****

Additional Kitchen Essentials

A Set of Kitchen Knives
Chopping Boards
Glass Storage Bowls with Lids
Mixing Bowls
Measuring Spoons and Cups
Colander and Strainer
Glass Mason Jars with Lids
Vegetable Peeler
Stainless Steel Pots and Pans
Salad Spinner

Breakfast

Cornbread Banana Walnut Pancakes

*A healthy breakfast is a great way
to start the day!*

Quick Fluffy Vegan Waffles

Prep time: 5 -10 mins
Cook Time: 1 min
Serving Size: 4 waffles

Ingredients:
- 1 ½ cups spelt flour
- 2 tablespoons turbinado or pure cane sugar
- 1 tablespoon baking powder
- 1 cup unsweetened vanilla almond milk
- 3 tablespoons grapeseed oil

Instructions:
- Preheat waffle maker and preheat oven to 200 degrees F (for keeping waffles warm).
- In a mixing bowl, combine the flour, sugar, baking powder, almond milk, and grapeseed oil. If too thick, add more milk. Mix well until most of the lumps are gone.
- Scoop up a ½ cup of batter and pour in the center of the heated waffle maker. Close the cover and cook according to manufacturer's instructions.
- When finished, gently remove and place on the cookie sheet and put in the oven to keep warm while making other waffles.

Simple Fluffy Pancakes

Prep time: 5 -10 mins
Cook Time: 10 mins
Serving Size: 6 to 8 pancakes

Ingredients:
- 1 cup spelt flour
- 2 tablespoons pure cane sugar
- 1 tablespoon baking powder, aluminum free
- ½ teaspoon sea salt
- 1 cup unsweetened almond milk
- 1 tablespoon apple cider vinegar
- 1 tablespoon vanilla

Instructions:
- In a medium bowl, add the flour, sugar, baking powder and salt. Stir and mix well.
- In a separate bowl, add milk, vinegar, and vanilla. Stir and mix well.
- Pour the liquid mixture into the dry mixture and whisk until smooth.
- Allow batter to sit for 3 to 5 minutes.
- In a nonstick skillet or griddle over medium heat, pour ¼ to ½ cup of batter.
- When the top begins to bubble, flip over, and cook until golden.
- Remove from heat and add to a paper towel lined plate and continue cooking next pancake.
- Serve with your choice of maple syrup.

Banana Walnut Cornbread Pancakes

Prep time: 5 -10 mins
Cook Time: 10 mins
Serving Size: 6 to 8 pancakes

Ingredients:
- 2 ripe bananas, mashed
- 1/3 cup pure cane sugar
- 1 tablespoon brown sugar
- 2 teaspoons vanilla extract
- 1 ½ cup unsweetened almond milk
- 2 cups organic cornmeal
- ¼ cup spelt flour
- ½ cup of walnuts, chopped
- 2 teaspoons cinnamon
- 1 teaspoon sea salt
- 2 teaspoons baking powder, aluminum free
- Vegan butter, for cooking

Instructions:
- In a large bowl, mash the bananas. Add both sugars and vanilla and whisk until mixed. Add milk and continue to combine. Set aside.
- In a separate bowl add cornmeal, flour, salt, baking powder, and cinnamon and whisk until all ingredients are blended well. Add to wet ingredients and mix well.
- Next, add walnuts and mix well.
- In a medium skillet or griddle over medium heat, melt 1 teaspoon butter and add 1/3 to ¼ cup of batter.
- Cook until lightly golden, then flip and continue to cook until other side is lightly golden.
- Remove from heat and transfer to a paper towel lined plate and continue with the remaining batter.
- Serve with agave or maple syrup.

Breakfast "Grab-n-Go" Chia Parfait

Prep time: 15 mins
Cook Time: 0 mins
Serving Size: 2

Ingredients:
- 1 large ripe mashed banana
- 2 tablespoons chia seeds
- ¼ teaspoon cinnamon spice
- ½ cup rolled oats
- ¾ cup unsweetened almond milk
- ¼ teaspoon pure vanilla extract

Toppings:
- Blueberries
- Strawberries
- Coconut Flakes
- Granola
- Nuts and Seeds

Instructions:
- Prepare ingredients the night before.
- In a medium bowl, mash the banana until almost smooth.
- Stir in the chia seeds and cinnamon until mixed.
- Add in the oats, almond milk, and vanilla. Mix well and pour mixture evenly into 2 (10 to 12 ounce) mason jars, cover and refrigerate overnight.
- In the morning, add your favorite toppings and enjoy.

Chickpea Breakfast Omelet

Prep time: 10 mins
Cook Time: 5 mins
Serving Size: 2

Chickpea Batter Ingredients:
- ¾ cup chickpea flour
- ¾ to 1 cup unsweetened almond milk
- 2 teaspoons apple cider vinegar
- 1 teaspoon nutritional yeast
- ¼ teaspoon turmeric powder
- ¼ teaspoon onion powder
- ¼ teaspoon garlic powder
- ¼ teaspoon baking soda
- Sea salt and pepper to taste
- Grapeseed oil for cooking

Omelet Ingredients:
- 1 to 2 cups spinach
- ¼ cup red onion, diced
- 1 tablespoon garlic, minced
- ¼ cup cherry or plum tomatoes, diced
- ¼ cup red bell pepper, diced
- ¼ cup green bell pepper, diced
- Vegetable broth to sauté

Instructions:
- In a bowl, mix all ingredients for the chickpea batter. The batter should be easy to pour like pancake batter.
- In a skillet, heat 2 tablespoons broth and sauté onion, bell peppers, and garlic until translucent or lightly browned.

Add tomatoes and spinach and sauté until spinach has softened. Remove from skillet and place on a plate.

- Return to the heated skillet, add a little oil and pour half of the batter into the pan. Add some of the omelet ingredients on the top half of the batter. When the batter begins to bubble and firms up along the edges, gently fold over one side to cook another minute. Cover with a lid and turn off the stove and allow to steam for 5 minutes.
- Garnish with more of the omelet ingredients and add salt and pepper to taste.

Eggless Scramble

Prep time: 5 min
Cook Time: 15 mins
Serving Size: 2

Ingredients:
- 1 cup garbanzo bean (chickpea) flour
- 1 cup water
- 3 tablespoons aquafaba* (liquid from a can of chickpeas)
- 2 tablespoons nutritional yeast
- ½ teaspoon turmeric
- ½ teaspoon cumin
- ½ teaspoon chili powder
- ¼ teaspoon sea salt
- ¼ teaspoon black pepper
- ¼ teaspoon kala namak* (black salt), optional

Veggies:
- ¼ onion, diced
- 1 garlic clove, minced
- ½ cup green pepper, diced
- 1 cup spinach, chopped
- 1 small plum tomato, diced
- 1 tablespoon grapeseed oil

Instructions:
- Combine all ingredients **EXCEPT** veggies in a bowl, mix well until there are no lumps. Set aside.
- Heat the grapeseed oil over medium heat and add onions and garlic. Stir constantly to avoid burning.
- Add green pepper when the onion starts to turn translucent; continue to stir.

- After pepper has softened, add spinach and tomatoes and stir for a minute longer.
- Pour the chickpea batter over the veggies while in the pan and allow to sit for about 2 minutes, sort of like you would an omelet.
- Next, scramble the mixture, scraping the bottom of the pan and allow it to sit, undisturbed for another 2 minutes before scrambling again. Continue until the dough begins to dry out.
- Turn off heat and allow the mixture to sit in the pan for 2 minutes

Aquafaba: *This is the liquid that is found in canned chickpeas.*

Kala Namak (Black Salt): *This salt adds an "eggy" flavor to the scramble.*

Lunch

This is a Chickpea Taco.

Time for Lunch!

Chickpea Tacos w/Creamy Sauce

Prep time: 10 mins
Cook Time: 5 mins
Serving Size: 4 to 6

Chickpea Taco Filling Ingredients:
- 2 (15-ounce cans) chickpeas, rinsed, drained & mashed
- Vegetable broth (used for sautéing)
- ¾ cup onion, chopped
- ½ cup green bell pepper, chopped
- 2 teaspoons chili powder
- 2 teaspoons ground cumin
- 2 teaspoons paprika
- 2 teaspoons garlic powder
- 1 teaspoon onion powder
- 1 teaspoon dried oregano
- 3 tablespoons lime juice, freshly squeezed
- ¾ sea salt

Creamy Taco Sauce:
- 1 small roma tomato, chopped
- 1 large avocado, pitted
- 2 tablespoons lime juice, freshly squeezed
- ¼ cup vegetable broth
- Sea salt to taste

Instructions for Chickpea Taco Filling:
- Heat vegetable broth in a skillet over medium-high heat. Add the onion, bell pepper, chili powder, cumin, paprika, garlic powder, onion powder, oregano, and salt. Sauté, stirring occasionally, for 5 to 7 minutes, until onion is transparent. You may need to add more vegetable broth to keep from drying out and sticking.

- Next, add the mashed chickpeas, lime juice, and stir thoroughly. Reduce the heat and simmer until chickpeas are heated through.

Instructions for Creamy Taco Sauce:
- Using a blender, add all ingredients until smooth and creamy. For a thinner sauce, add extra broth.

Add taco filling to a soft- or hard-shell taco with lettuce and chopped tomatoes; then, top with the creamy taco sauce. Enjoy!

Quinoa Veggie Bowl w/Maple Dressing

Prep time: 20 mins
Cook Time: 15 -20 min
Serving Size: 2 to 4 small bowls

Ingredients:
- 2 cups quinoa, cooked
- 2 large carrots, sliced
- 1 large head broccoli florets, chopped
- 1 red bell pepper, chopped
- ½ small head red cabbage, sliced
- 2 tablespoons grapeseed oil
- 1 teaspoon garlic powder
- 1 teaspoon onion powder
- ½ teaspoon sea salt
- ½ teaspoon black pepper

Maple Dressing:
- ¼ cup Bragg's liquid aminos
- 2 tablespoons pure maple syrup
- 1 teaspoon ginger, minced
- 1 teaspoon garlic, minced

Instructions:
- Preheat oven to 425 degrees.
- Line a baking sheet with parchment paper, set aside.
- In a medium bowl, combine oil, garlic powder, onion powder, salt, and black pepper. Mix well.
- Add each batch of vegetables and season with oil and spices. Then, place on a baking sheet. You will have four batches of seasoned vegetables.
- Bake in the oven for 15 – 20 minutes, or until roasted to your liking.

- Fill 2 to 4 small bowls with 1/2 cup cooked quinoa. Then, fill with roasted vegetables
- Add maple dressing and enjoy!

Chickpea Veggie Bowl w/Cilantro Dressing

Prep time: 20 mins
Cook Time: 15 -20 min
Serving Size: 2 to 4 small bowls

Ingredients:
- 2 cups brown rice, cooked
- 1 sweet potato, peeled and quartered
- ½ pound brussels sprouts, trimmed and halved
- 1 yellow bell pepper, chopped
- ½ red onion, chopped
- 1 15 ounce can chickpeas, drained and rinsed
- 2 tablespoons grapeseed oil
- 1 ½ teaspoons paprika
- ½ teaspoon sea salt
- ½ teaspoon black pepper

Cilantro Dressing:
- ¼ cup So Delicious Plain Vegan Yogurt
- 2 tablespoons lime juice, fresh squeezed
- 1 tablespoon fresh cilantro, chopped
- 1 teaspoon garlic, minced
- 1 teaspoon ginger, minced

Instructions:
- Preheat oven to 425 degrees.
- Line a baking sheet with parchment paper, set aside.
- In a medium bowl, combine oil, paprika, salt, and black pepper. Mix well.
- Add each batch of vegetables and season with oil and spices. Then, place on a baking sheet. You will have five batches of seasoned vegetables.

- Bake in the oven for 15 – 20 minutes, or until roasted to your liking.
- Fill 2 to 4 small bowls with 1 cup cooked brown rice. Then, fill with roasted vegetables
- Add cilantro dressing and enjoy!

Curried Chickpea Salad

Prep time: 10 mins
Cook Time: 0 mins
Serving Size: 4

Ingredients:
- ½ cup vegan mayo
- ½ teaspoon curry powder
- 1 15 ounce can chickpeas, rinsed and drained
- 1 medium carrot, shredded
- 1 small apple, cored and chopped
- 1 to 2 tablespoons red onion, chopped

Instructions:
In a large bowl, mash the Chickpeas. Then, add mayo and curry powder and mix well. Stir in the carrots, apples, and onions.

Broccoli Walnut Salad

Prep time: 10 mins
Cook Time: 0 mins
Serving Size: 4

Ingredients:
- 3 cups broccoli florets
- ½ cup raisins
- ½ cup red onion, chopped
- ½ cup walnuts, chopped
- 1 tablespoon pure raw cane sugar
- 2 -3 tablespoons apple cider vinegar
- ½ - ¾ cup vegan mayo

Instructions:
- In a large salad bowl, add broccoli, raisins, onion, and walnuts.
- In a separate bowl, mix sugar, vinegar, and mayo. Feel free to adjust.
- Add dressing mixture to the broccoli and toss to mix.

Garden Vegetable Soup

Prep time: 30 mins
Cook Time: 35 mins
Serving Size: 4 to 5

Ingredients:
- 3 tablespoons – vegetable broth
- 1 1/2 cups chopped yellow onion
- 2 cups peeled and chopped carrots
- 1 1/4 cups chopped celery
- 4 cloves garlic, minced
- 4 cups vegetable broth
- 2 (14.5 ounces) cans diced tomatoes (undrained)
- 3 cups peeled and 1/2-inch thick diced potatoes (from about 3 medium)
- 1/3 cup chopped fresh parsley
- 2 bay leaves
- ½ teaspoon dried thyme
- Salt and freshly ground black pepper
- 1 ½ cups chopped frozen or fresh green beans
- 1 ¼ cups frozen or fresh organic corn (optional)
- 1 cup frozen or fresh peas

Instructions:
- Heat 3 to 4 tablespoons vegetable broth in a large pot over medium heat.
- Add onions, carrots, and celery and sauté 4 minutes then add garlic and sauté 30 seconds longer. You may need to add more broth. Make sure broth doesn't dissolve.
- Add in 4 cups broth, tomatoes, potatoes, parsley, bay leaves, thyme and season with salt and pepper to taste (for more flavor add in more dried herbs as desired).
- Bring to a boil, and then add green beans.

- Reduce heat to medium-low, cover and simmer until potatoes are tender, about 20 - 30 minutes, then add corn and peas and cook 5 minutes longer.
- Serve warm and enjoy!

Vegan Cheesesteak Sandwiches

Prep time: 10 mins
Cook Time: 15 mins
Serving Size: 2

Ingredients:
- 1 pkg Seitan
- 1 medium onion, cut into strips
- ½ green bell pepper, cut into strips
- ½ red bell pepper, cut into strips
- Salt and pepper to season
- Avocado oil for sautéing
- 2 hoagie buns

Homemade Cheese Sauce Ingredients:
- 2 tablespoons grapeseed oil
- 1/3 cup all-purpose unbleached flour
- ½ teaspoon sea salt
- 1/8 teaspoon turmeric powder
- ¼ teaspoon curry powder
- ¼ teaspoon paprika powder
- 1/3 cup nutritional yeast
- ½ cup water

Instructions:
- In a large skillet with 1 tablespoon avocado oil, sauté onion, green and red bell peppers until soft or onion is translucent. Add seitan and continue cooking for 1 to 2 minutes. Set aside.
- Next, prepare the cheesy sauce. Heat the oil in a small pot over low heat. Add the salt, turmeric powder, curry powder, and paprika powder. Add the flour and whisk. Add nutritional yeast, and whisk again. Add the water

and continue to whisk on low heat until it becomes gooey. Put in blender, and blend until smooth.

- Fill hoagies with seitan.
- Add lettuce, tomatoes, and cheese sauce on top. Enjoy!

Oven-Fried Zucchini Coins

Prep time: 10 mins
Cook Time: 15 mins
Serving Size: 4

Ingredients:

- 3 medium zucchinis, cut into round slices
- ¼ cup unsweetened almond milk
- ½ cup chickpea flour
- 2 tablespoons nutritional yeast
- 1 teaspoon Italian seasoning
- ¼ teaspoon salt

Homemade Ranch Dipping Sauce:

- 1 cup vegan mayo
- ½ cup unsweetened almond milk
- ½ tablespoon garlic powder
- ½ tablespoon onion powder
- ¼ teaspoon black pepper
- 2 teaspoons dried parsley
- ½ teaspoon lemon juice
- 1 teaspoon dill

Instructions:

- Preheat oven to 400 degrees
- For the "Ranch Dipping Sauce," combine and mix all ingredients. Set aside
- Cut zucchinis into sliced circular rounds and place in a large mixing bowl. Pour almond milk into the bowl and mix well.
- Combine chickpea flour, nutritional yeast, and seasonings in a different bowl. Remove zucchini from milk bowl and add to "flour" bowl to evenly coat.

- Distribute onto a baking sheet and bake for 15 minutes. Flip and bake for an addition 5 to 6 minutes until golden brown.
- Serve with homemade ranch dipping sauce.

Raw Nut Tacos

Prep time: 10 mins
Cook Time: 0 mins
 Serving Size: 4

Ingredients:
- Savoy cabbage or romaine lettuce (whole, not in bag)
- 1 medium avocado, sliced thin

Nut Meat Ingredients:
- 1/3 cup raw pecans
- 1/3 cup raw sunflower seeds
- ¾ teaspoon turmeric powder
- ¾ teaspoon cumin powder
- 1 ½ teaspoons tamari

Salsa Ingredients:
- ½ cup diced cherry or roma tomatoes
- ½ cup organic yellow or blue corn (omit any juice)
- 1 lime, squeezed
- 2 basil leaves, finely chopped
- ¼ cup of diced red onions

Instructions:
- Separate the romaine lettuce leaves or the savoy cabbage leaves – they should look like shells
- For the nut meat – add all ingredients to a small food chopper and grind for less than a minute.
- For the salsa – (in a separate bowl) mix all ingredients.

You are now ready to make "Tacos!" Enjoy!

Mushroom Po Boy Sandwich

Prep time: 40 mins
Cook Time: 5 mins
Serving Size: 4

Sauce Ingredients:
- 1 cup vegan mayo
- 2 tablespoons BBQ sauce
- 1 tablespoon mustard
- 1 tablespoon dried parsley
- 1 tablespoon garlic, minced
- ½ teaspoon white pepper
- 1 teaspoon vegan horseradish
- 1 tablespoon lemon juice
- 1 teaspoon vegan Worcestershire sauce
- ½ teaspoon Old Bay seasoning
- 1 teaspoon sea salt

Mushroom Ingredients:
- A large package of oyster mushrooms cleaned cut in small pieces
- ½ cup unsweetened almond milk
- 2 tablespoons ground flax seed powder
- 5 to 6 tablespoons water
- 1 cup cornmeal
- ½ tablespoon garlic powder
- ½ tablespoon onion powder
- 1 teaspoon paprika
- 1 teaspoon black pepper
- Grapeseed oil for frying

Instructions:
- For the sauce, combine and mix all "Sauce" ingredients until smooth. Set aside.
- Next, mix the flaxseed powder and water in a small bowl. Set aside for 5 to 10 minutes. This is called a flax egg and is used to help batter the mushrooms.
- In a different bowl, combine and mix the DRY ingredients: cornmeal, powders, paprika, pepper. Separate the washed mushroom into small pieces and make sure there's no water by squeezing the mushrooms. Add the almond milk to the flaxseed mixture and stir well.
- Heat up 1 to 2 cups of Grapeseed oil in a deep fryer or skillet.
- Dip the mushroom pieces in the milk/flax mixture, then, the cornmeal mixture and add to the fryer for cooking.
- Cook mushrooms for 1 to 2 minutes. Then, place on paper towels to drain. Continue until all mushrooms have been cooked.

You can now make your sandwich by using a hoagie bun, lettuce, sliced tomatoes, sliced pickles, onion, and sauce. Enjoy!

Fried Green Tomatoes w/Aioli Sauce

Prep time: 15 mins
Cook Time: 5 mins
 Serving Size: 4

Ingredients:
Fried Green Tomatoes:
- 4 to 5 green tomatoes, cleaned and sliced
- ½ cup cornmeal
- ½ cup chickpea (garbanzo) flour
- ½ cup unsweetened almond milk
- 1 ½ teaspoons apple cider vinegar
- 1 tablespoon ground flaxseed
- 3 tablespoons water
- 1 tablespoon Creole seasoning
- Avocado oil for frying

Aioli Sauce:
- ½ cup vegan mayo
- ¼ cup vegan sour cream
- ½ cup roasted red peppers
- 1 tablespoon garlic powder
- 2 teaspoons dried basil
- Sea salt and pepper to taste

Instructions for Aioli Sauce:
- Make the sauce first. Simply add all ingredients to a blender or food processor and mix until smooth. Refrigerate until ready.

Instructions for Fried Green Tomatoes:
- In a bowl, add almond milk and vinegar, mix and allow to sit for a few minutes. In a smaller bowl, add water and

the ground flaxseed and mix. This will become a binder. Let sit for 1 minute or two, then, add to almond milk mixture.

- Cut tomatoes into ½ inch slices. Set aside. Next, in a shallow bowl, combine the cornmeal, flour, and seasoning.
- Dip the tomato slices into the milk/flaxseed mixture, and now you can batter the tomato slices using the flour/cornmeal mixture.
- Fry until golden brown on both sides. Remove from oil and place on lined paper towel.
- Serve with aioli sauce.

Vegetable Spring Rolls with Sauce

Prep Time: 15 mins
Cooking Time: 10 mins
Serving Size: 4

Ingredients:
Rolls:

- 1 ½ cup cabbage, shredded
- 2 medium carrots, julienned
- ½ cup bean sprouts
- ½ cup green onions, finely chopped
- 1 tablespoon of cilantro
- 2 tablespoons tamari sauce
- 4 garlic cloves, minced
- 8 sheets of spring pastry rolls
- Avocado oil
- Sea salt and pepper to taste

Sauce Ingredients:

- 2 tablespoons ketchup
- 2 teaspoons tamari sauce
- 3 tablespoons rice vinegar
- 4 tablespoons agave syrup
- 1 teaspoon pineapple juice – optional
- 1/3 cup water
- 3 teaspoons cornstarch

Instructions for Rolls:

- Heat at medium-high 1 tablespoon of oil in a skillet or wok, add cabbage, carrots, sprouts, onions, and garlic. Stir frequently and continue to sauté until carrots and cabbage are soft (about 2 minutes).

- Add the cilantro, tamari sauce, salt, and pepper and continue to sauté for another minute or 2. Remove from heat.
- Place a spring roll wrapper on a flat surface, add a small amount of the cooked vegetable mixer into a corner of the wrapper, then roll the edge of the wrapper tightly around the mixture. Fold the left and the right sides toward the middle of the wrapper while rolling up. Brush a small amount of water to the top edge to seal. Place seam side down.
- In a deep fryer or large skillet over high heat, add ½ to 1 cup of oil. Slowly add spring rolls to oil and cook until both sides are browned.
- Place on a cooling rack or paper towel covered plate to allow to drain.

Instructions for Sauce:
- In a small bowl, add water and cornstarch and mix well. Set aside.
- In another bowl, mix ketchup, tamari, rice vinegar, agave syrup, and pineapple.
- In a saucepan over medium-high heat, add both mixtures and cook until it thickens. Stir occasionally. Remove and let the sauce cool.

Cauliflower and Mushroom Quesadillas

Prep time: 10 mins
Cook Time: 15 mins
Serving Size: 6

Ingredients for Quesadillas:
- 1 medium cauliflower head, cut in halves
- 2/3 cups or 5 ounces baby Bella mushrooms
- ½ medium yellow onion, diced
- ¼ cup green bell pepper, chopped
- ¼ cup red bell pepper, chopped
- 2 garlic cloves, minced
- 2 teaspoons ground cumin
- 1 teaspoon paprika
- ½ teaspoon chipotle powder
- 2 tablespoons chili powder
- 1 teaspoon garlic powder
- 1 teaspoon onion powder
- 2 tablespoons liquid amino (soy sauce alternative)
- 1 package flour tortillas
- 1 package vegan shredded cheese blend
- 1 tablespoon cilantro
- Avocado Oil

Ingredients for Avocado Lime Sauce:
- 1 small avocado, pitted and mashed
- 1 tablespoon roasted red bell peppers
- ½ cup vegan sour cream
- ¼ cup vegan mayo
- ¼ cup freshly chopped cilantro
- 1 lime, juiced

Instructions for Quesadillas:
- Cut the cauliflower into halves and place in a food processor and pulse until they are rice-sizes pieces. Remove from processor and set aside.
- Place mushrooms in the food processor and pulse until they are rice-size pieces. Remove from processor and set aside.
- Heat 1 tablespoon of oil in a large skillet over medium heat. Add onion, green bell pepper, red bell pepper, and garlic and sauté until onion is translucent.
- Add the cauliflower, mushrooms, cumin, paprika, chili powder, chipotle powder, Bragg's liquid amino, garlic powder, and onion powder. Cook for about 8 minutes, until the cauliflower and mushroom mixture is tender. Set aside.
- In a separate skillet, add ½ teaspoon oil over low heat and heat tortilla. Sprinkle half of the tortilla with cheese, then add a layer of cauliflower mixture over the cheese, then add another layer of cheese.
- Fold tortilla and cook for amount 3 minutes, then, flip over and cook for an additional 2 or 3 minutes. Remove from skillet and slice in half. Repeat.

Instructions for Sauce:
Combine all ingredients in a small blender and blend until smooth. Serve over quesadillas or use as a dipping sauce.

Raw Vegetable Spring Rolls

Prep time: 40 mins
Cook Time: 0 mins
Serving Size: 4

Ingredients for Rolls:
- 1 yellow or red bell pepper, cut into strips
- 2 leaves red cabbage, cut into strips
- 2 cups of spinach
- 1 to 2 carrots, julienned
- 1 cucumber, julienned
- 8 brown rice paper rounds

Ingredients for Sauce:
- ½ cup raw soak cashews
- 1 carrot, cut into slices
- 1 lemon or lime juiced
- 1 teaspoon mild curry spice
- 1 teaspoon turmeric

Instructions for Rolls:
- Soak cashews for 30 minutes to an hour. Do not discard water.
- Set all prepared vegetables aside.
- Next, in a medium bowl add warm water
- Dip the rice paper into the water until it softens. Remove and lay on a flat surface.
- Near the bottom of the paper, lay a small amount of spinach first. Then, top with bell pepper, cucumber, carrots, and red cabbage.
- Fold in the left and the right sides of the paper, then pull bottom edge over the vegetables and roll the paper

tightly away from you until it is closed. Set aside and repeat with the remaining paper and vegetable fillings.

Instructions for Sauce:
- Add all ingredients, including the water used to soak cashews and blend until creamy.
- Use sauce to dip spring rolls.

Kelp Noodles with Almond Butter Sauce

Prep time: 15 mins
Cook Time: 0 mins
Serving Size: 2

Ingredients for Kelp Noodles:
- 1 (12 ounce) package of kelp noodles
- 1 cup organic baby spinach, diced
- ½ cup red bell pepper, cut into small strips
- ½ cup yellow bell pepper, cut into small strips
- 1 cucumber, julienned
- 8 brown rice paper rounds

Ingredients for Noodle Sauce:
- 1 can (15 to 16 ounces) coconut milk
- ½ cup of almond butter or peanut butter
- 1 tablespoon extra-virgin cold-pressed olive oil
- 1 tablespoon cilantro
- 2 garlic cloves, minced
- 1 teaspoon sea salt
- 1 jalapeno, diced - optional

Instructions for Sauce:
- Remove kelp noodles from the package and rinse. Set aside.
- After preparing vegetables. Set aside.
- Next, prepare the sauce. Add all ingredients, except jalapeno, and blend until creamy and smooth.
- In a medium bowl, add kelp noodles and vegetables, then, pour the sauce over noodles and vegetables.
- Mix well and enjoy.

Boneless Vegan Wings

Breakfast "Grab-n-Go"
Chia Parfait

No Squidding Calamari

Vegan Cinnamon Rolls

Fried Green Tomatoes
w/Aioli Sauce

Raw Nut Tacos

Easy Like Sunday
Morning Peach Cobbler

Mushroom Po Boy
Sandwich

"No-Cook" Stir Fry
w/Cauliflower Rice

Cashew Ricotta Shells
w/Spinach

Spaghetti with
Cauliflower and
Mushroom Sauce

Simple Spring Rolls
with Sauce

Easy Stuffed Taco Bell Peppers

Vegetable Beefless Stew

Dinner

54

Lasagna! Lasagna!

Dinner is better when it's healthy!

Vegetable Couscous w/Sausage

Prep time: 15 mins
Cook Time: 20 mins
Serving Size: 6

Ingredients:
- 1 pkg Field Roast Italian Sausage
- 1 tablespoon grapeseed oil
- 1 medium onion, chopped
- 1 red bell pepper, seeded and chopped
- 2 tablespoons garlic, minced
- 1 cup cherry tomatoes, halved
- ½ cup green onions, sliced
- 1 ½ cups vegetable broth
- 1 cup couscous, plain
- 2 tablespoons fresh lemon juice
- 2 tablespoons fresh parsley, chopped

Instructions:
- Cut sausage into ½-inch slices. Add grapeseed oil and sausage to a large skillet (non-stick) Cook and stir over medium heat for 2 -3 minutes or until lightly browned.
- Stir in onion, peppers, and garlic; cook and stir for 2-3 minutes stirring or until vegetables are tender. Add tomatoes, green onion, and vegetable broth.
- Increase heat to medium-high and bring the liquid to a boil. Stir in couscous. Remove from heat and let sit for 5 minutes.
- Stir in lemon juice and sprinkle with parsley before serving.
- Enjoy!

Boneless Vegan Wings

Prep time: 25 mins
Cook Time: 15 -20 mins
Serving Size: 4

Ingredients:
- 1 cup Vital Wheat Gluten
- 2 tablespoons nutritional yeast
- 1 teaspoon onion powder
- 1 teaspoon garlic powder
- 1 teaspoon paprika
- ½ teaspoon sea salt
- ½ teaspoon poultry seasoning
- ¾ cup vegetable broth
- 2 tablespoons tahini

Batter:
- 2 eggs worth of egg replacer (follow instructions on box)
- 1 to 2 tablespoons hot sauce
- ½ teaspoon black pepper
- 2 cups all-purpose unbleached flour
- ½ tablespoon garlic power

Instructions for Chick'n Meat:
- Preheat oven to 350 degrees.
- In a medium bowl, combine vital wheat gluten, nutritional yeast, onion powder, garlic powder, paprika, salt, and poultry seasoning and mix well. Set aside
- In a separate bowl, combine ¾ cup broth and tahini and whisk until well blended.
- Mix the dry and the wet ingredients until well combined.

- Knead the dough until it's elastic but not dry. If too sticky, add more flour.
- Divide the dough into small little "chick'n" wing pieces. Note: make them smaller because they will double in size. Next, place them in a casserole dish and cover them with vegetable broth.
- Bake wings in the broth for 30 to 45 minutes, flipping after 25 minutes. Allow to cool.

Instructions for Batter:
- In a bowl, whisk together the egg replacer, hot sauce, and garlic powder.
- Put flour and black pepper in a Ziplock bag or a different bowl.
- Dredge the chick'n wings into the egg mixture them toss in the flour mixture.
- Deep fry in a deep fryer or large pot of heated oil for 3 to 5 minutes. Remove wings; place on a paper towel lined plate.
- Use vegan ranch sauce to dip wings. Enjoy.

Vegetable Beefless Stew

Prep time: 30 mins
Cook Time: 40-45 mins
Serving Size: 6

Ingredients:
- 2 large white potatoes, peeled and cut into cubes
- 2 large carrots, cut into slices
- 1 large yellow onion, chopped
- 3 celery stalks, chopped
- 2 portabella mushrooms, cut into pieces
- 2 tablespoons garlic, minced
- 4 to 5 cups vegetable broth
- ¼ cup tomato paste
- 1 tablespoon paprika
- 2 teaspoons rosemary spice
- 1 tablespoon Italian herb seasoning
- 1 vegetable bouillon cube
- ½ tablespoon parsley

Instructions:
- In a large pot, heat 2 tablespoons of vegetable broth over medium heat, add onions, carrots, and celery, stirring often, add more broth as needed.
- Stir in the mushrooms and garlic and continue cooking while stirring for at least 5 minutes, add more broth as needed.
- Add cups of broth, potatoes, tomato paste, Italian seasoning, paprika, and vegetable bouillon, bring to a boil, uncovered.
- Reduce the heat to medium-low and add the rosemary. Cover and cook for 25 to 30 minutes, or until the carrots and potatoes are tender.

- Place 2 cups of the stew, both vegetables, and broth into a blender, and blend briefly. Stir the mixture back into the pot. This will thicken the stew. Stir in parsley.

Note: This is a great dish to serve over quinoa or brown rice with cornbread.

Creamy Broccoli, Rice and Mushroom Casserole

Prep time: 30 mins
Cook Time: 40-45 mins
Serving Size: 6

Sauce Ingredients:
- 1 ¼ cup, unsweetened almond milk creamer
- ½ cup nutritional yeast
- 4 teaspoons cornstarch
- 1 garlic clove, minced
- ½ tablespoon lemon juice
- ½ teaspoon sea salt
- ½ teaspoon onion powder
- ¼ teaspoon mustard
- ¼ teaspoon smoked paprika
- 1 tablespoon tahini
- ¼ teaspoon black pepper

Casserole Ingredients:
- 1 large head broccoli, cut into small florets
- 1 medium onion, chopped
- ½ red bell pepper, chopped
- ½ cup celery, chopped
- 1 cup chickpeas, cooked (optional)
- 1 teaspoon dried thyme
- 2 cups brown rice, cooked
- Vegetable broth for steaming and sautéing

Instructions:
- Preheat oven 375 degrees. Lightly oil or spray a medium casserole dish.

- Place the sauce ingredients into a blender and process until smooth. Set aside.
- Place broccoli in a medium pot, add ½ cup vegetable broth, cover until tender. Remove from heat.
- Heat a large pot with ¼ cup of vegetable broth and add the onion, bell pepper, celery and sauté for 3 to 4 minutes. Stir in the chickpeas, rice, steamed broccoli, and thyme. Pour in the sauce mixture.
- Add all ingredients into the prepared casserole dish, cover and bake for 25 – 30 minutes or until slightly golden.

Easy Chili

Prep time: 5 mins
Cook Time: 35 mins
Serving Size: 6

Ingredients:
- Vegan crumbles – optional
- ½ teaspoon sea salt
- ½ teaspoon black pepper
- 1 tablespoon chili powder
- 1 small onion, chopped
- 1 garlic clove, minced
- ½ cup green bell pepper, chopped
- 1 bay leaf
- 1 (28 ounce) can diced tomatoes with liquid
- 1 (14 ounce) can tomato sauce
- 1 (16 ounce) can kidney beans with liquid
- Vegetable broth

Instructions:
- In a large soup pot, heat 3 tablespoons of vegetable broth over medium heat, add onions, bell pepper, garlic and sauté until translucent. Add vegan crumbles and continue to sauté. You may need to add more broth. Then, all add spices and stir for at least another minute.
- Add all other ingredients and simmer for at least 30 minutes.
- Enjoy!

Lasagna! Lasagna!

Prep time: 30 mins
Cook Time: 40 - 45 mins
Serving Size: 6 to 8

Lasagna Ingredients:
- Earth Balance vegan butter
- 1 box organic lasagna
- 1 package Field Roast Italian vegetarian sausage, chopped
- 8 ounces Kite Hill ricotta cheese
- 1 bag Daiya mozzarella cheese
- 1 head organic broccoli
- 1 large organic yellow squash
- 1 bunch of organic spinach

Sauce Ingredients:
- ¼ cup grapeseed oil
- ¾ teaspoon black mustard seeds
- ½ teaspoon ground turmeric
- ¼ teaspoon coriander
- ¼ teaspoon fenugreek
- ¼ teaspoon ground cumin
- 2 plum tomatoes, chopped
- 2 large jars pasta sauce
- 1/3 cup tomato paste
- 2 tablespoons Organic Blackstrap Molasses
- 1 ½ teaspoons Italian herb blend
- 1 ½ teaspoons sea salt

Instructions:
- **Sauce Instructions**: In a large saucepan, on medium, heat the oil. Add the mustard seeds, turmeric, coriander,

fenugreek, cumin, and stir and cook until the mustard seeds begin to pop (about 2 minutes). Add tomatoes and continue to stir until soft. Next, add tomato sauce and paste and lower heat to simmer for about 5 minutes. Stir in molasses, Italian herbs, salt and simmer for another minute. Set aside.

- Prepare the lasagna according to the directions on the package.
- Heat a tablespoon of butter in a large skillet over medium heat. Add the chopped sausage and cook until browned. Transfer to a large bowl and allow to cool.
- Once the sausage has cooled, stir in the ricotta and ¼ cup of mozzarella. Set aside.
- Next, cook broccoli and squash in a large pot of water until tender. Drain and lightly mash or chop the vegetable.
- Heat the oven to 350 degrees. Grease bottom of a casserole dish with butter; then, layer the bottom with a few sheets of cooked lasagna. Top with 1/3 of the "sausage" mixture and spread into an even layer; spread about a cup of pasta sauce over the sausage; then top with 1/3 of the vegetables and 1/3 of the spinach. Top with ½ cup of the mozzarella cheese and pasta sauce. Top with another layer of pasta and repeat steps. End with a layer of pasta on top of the remaining sauce. Cover with aluminum foil and bake for 30 minutes. Remove the foil and top with remaining mozzarella cheese and bake an additional 10 to 15 minutes.

Easy Stuffed Taco Bell Peppers

Prep time: 10 min
Cook Time: 25 - 30 mins
Serving Size: 8

Ingredients:

- 4 large red bell peppers, sliced in half lengthwise and de-seeded
- 2 cups brown rice, cooked
- 1 pkg Gardein beefless grounds - optional
- 15 ounce can black beans, drained and rinsed
- 2 tablespoons grapeseed oil
- 16 ounces organic salsa
- 1 cup organic corn (non-GMO), drained and rinsed
- 2 cups vegan Mexican cheese shreds
- 1 pkg Simply Organic Mild Taco Seasoning Mix
- Sour cream
- Diced plum tomatoes with cilantro (optional)

Instructions:

- Preheat oven 350 degrees. Line a baking sheet with parchment paper.
- Place the peppers on the baking sheet. Set aside.
- In a large skillet on medium heat add oil and cook grounds until browned.
- Prepare taco seasoning according to contents and add to grounds.
- Together in a large bowl, mix the grounds, black beans, salsa, corn, rice, and a cup of cheese.
- Add the mixture to each pepper. Bake for 30 minutes. Add more cheese, if you like, and bake for five additional minutes.

- When ready to serve, top with Tofutti sour cream and diced tomatoes with cilantro.

Creamy Linguini Vegetable Alfredo

Prep time: 5 mins
Cook Time: 15 mins
Serving Size: 4

Ingredients:
- 1 pkg organic linguini
- 3 to 4 tablespoons vegetable broth
- 4 tablespoons garlic, minced
- 4 tablespoons all-purpose unbleached flour
- 1 to 2 cups unsweetened almond milk
- ¼ cup green bell pepper, chopped
- ¼ cup red bell pepper, chopped
- ¼ cup yellow onion, chopped
- 4 tablespoons nutritional yeast
- 1 teaspoon garlic powder
- ¼ cup vegan parmesan cheese
- Celtic sea salt to taste

Instructions:
- Cook linguini according to package. Drain, rinse in cold water – put back in the pot and set aside.
- In a large skillet, over medium heat, add vegetable broth and sauté onions and peppers for 1 to 2 minutes (you might need to add more broth). Set aside.
- In a different skillet, add vegetable broth and sauté garlic. Reduce heat and add flour and whisk to combine. Add ¼ cup of milk at a time (keep adding slowly) and continue to whisk to prevent clumps. Cook for approximately 2 minutes.
- Transfer garlic mixture to a blender. Add salt, parmesan cheese, nutritional yeast, garlic powder, and blend until creamy. If too thick, add more almond milk.

- Return sauce to the skillet and cook on medium heat until it bubbles.
- Add to pot of linguini and stir until coated.
- Serve with a nice small green salad.

Cashew Ricotta Shells w/Spinach

Prep time: 25 mins
Cook Time: 30 mins
Serving Size: 4

Ingredients:

- 2 cups raw cashews, soaked in water 3-4 hours
- ¼ cup unsweetened plain almond milk
- 3 tablespoons nutritional yeast
- 1 tablespoon garlic, minced
- 1 tablespoon lemon juice, fresh squeezed
- ¼ teaspoon sea salt
- ½ teaspoon ground black pepper
- ½ tablespoon dried basil
- ½ tablespoon dried oregano
- 1 tablespoon vegetable broth
- 1 box Tinkyada brown rice pasta shells, cooked, drained and rinsed in cold water
- 1 (25-ounce) jar marinara sauce
- 2 cups baby spinach
- ½ cup vegan parmesan cheese, shredded

Instructions:

- Preheat oven 350 degrees.
- Cook box of pasta shells according to directions.
- Next, drain and rinse cashews. Transfer them to a blender or a food processor. Combine milk, nutritional yeast, garlic, lemon juice, salt, black pepper, basil, and oregano. Process until blended well. You may need to use a plastic spatula to scrape the sides between blending. Place cashew mixture in a bowl and set aside.
- In a pan over low-medium heat, warm vegetable broth and sauté baby spinach until wilted. Make sure there's

no excess broth. Add to the bowl with the cashew mixture and mix well.

- Next, pour ½ of the jar of marinara over the bottom of a baking dish. Using a spoon, scoop the cashew mixture into each cooked shell then place in the baking dish.
- Spoon the remaining marinara on top of each shell, then cover the dish with foil and bake in the oven for 25 to 30 minutes.
- Top with fresh parsley, serve warm with small garden salad and enjoy!

Fried Mushrooms

Prep time: 10 mins
Cook Time: 30 mins
Serving Size: 8

Ingredients:
- ¾ - 1 cup unsweetened coconut milk
- 1 tablespoon lemon juice, fresh-squeezed
- 1 cup all-purpose unbleached flour
- ½ tablespoon cornstarch
- ½ teaspoon sea salt
- ½ teaspoon garlic powder
- ½ teaspoon onion powder
- ½ teaspoon paprika
- 1 to 2 tablespoons hot sauce
- 4 cups All-Natural Panko Breadcrumbs
- Pkg of cremini or white mushrooms, sliced in half
- Grapeseed oil for frying

Dipping Sauce Ingredients (optional):
- 1/2 cup hot sauce
- 4 tablespoons vegan butter
- 2 tablespoons organic ketchup or agave
- ½ cup Organicville BBQ Sauce

Instructions for Mushrooms:
- In a bowl, combine ¾ cup of milk, lemon juice, and hot sauce. Stir well until combined. Set aside.
- In a mixing bowl whisk together the flour, cornstarch, salt, garlic powder, onion powder, and paprika.
- Next, stir in the milk and lemon juice mixture and hot sauce. The batter should be thick (but a little runny) like pancake batter, if not, add more milk.

- In a different bowl, add breadcrumbs. Dip the mushroom in the batter first, then the breadcrumbs.
- Pour grapeseed oil into a deep fryer or use a skillet on the stove. When heated, fry the mushrooms in small batches for 1 to 2 ½ minutes on each side until golden brown and crispy. Drain on paper towels.
- Once the mushrooms have been fried, serve hot with a dipping sauce of your choice.

Instructions for Sauce:
In a saucepan over medium heat, melt butter. Add all other ingredients and simmer for approximately 2 minutes. Set aside.

Curried Vegetable Pot w/Spinach

Prep time: 10 mins
Cook Time: 35 mins
Serving Size: 4

Ingredients:
- 1 medium onion, chopped
- 2 carrots, chopped in slices
- 1 medium potato, chopped
- ½ cup of green bell pepper, chopped
- ½ cup of red bell pepper, chopped
- 2 garlic cloves, minced
- 1 tablespoon vegetable broth (used to sauté veggies)
- 2 tablespoon curry spice (mild or spicy)
- 1 teaspoon turmeric
- 1 teaspoon ginger
- 1 teaspoon cumin
- 1 teaspoon chili powder
- 1 teaspoon paprika
- 1 teaspoon cilantro
- ½ teaspoon cinnamon
- 1 cup coconut milk
- 2 bay leaves
- 1 can (15-ounces) chickpeas
- 1 bag of spinach
- Sea salt to season - optional

Instructions:
- In a large soup pot, sauté onion, green, and red bell peppers using the vegetable broth and add the curry spice once the onion is translucent.
- Using the same pot, add the carrots, garlic, and all spices and sauté for another minute or two. Now, add the

coconut milk. Let simmer for about 5 minutes but keep stirring to make sure it doesn't stick to the pot.
- Next, add the bay leaves, potatoes and the entire can of chickpeas with liquid. Allow to simmer for about 20 - 30 minutes.
- Add Spinach last and simmer until spinach has cooked.

"No-Cook" Stir Fry w/Cauliflower Rice

Prep time: 15 mins
Cook Time: 0 mins
Serving Size: 4

Marinade Ingredients:
- ½ cup grapeseed or olive oil
- 2 teaspoons sesame oil
- Juice of one lime
- 4 tablespoons tamari
- 2 tablespoons garlic, minced
- ¼ cup peanuts, diced
- 2 tablespoons fresh ginger, finely chopped

Vegetables:
- 2 cups broccoli florets, chopped
- 1 medium red bell pepper, seeded and sliced thin
- 1 cup carrots, julienned
- 1 cup bean sprouts
- ½ cup Bok Choy, shredded
- ½ cup savoy cabbage, shredded
- ½ medium red onion, diced

Cauliflower Rice:
- 3 cups cauliflower florets
- ½ cup unsweetened coconut, shredded
- ½ teaspoon Himalayan pink or Celtic sea salt

Instructions:
- For the marinade, place all ingredients in a high-speed blender until well combined. Pour into a large mixing bowl.

- Add all vegetables into the same bowl. Toss and allow vegetables to marinate while making cauliflower rice.
- For the coconut-cauliflower rice, pulse all ingredients in a food processor until cauliflower resembles the texture of rice. Don't over-process.
- Serve veggie mixture over cauliflower rice. Enjoy!

Raw Organic Zucchini Alfredo

Prep time: 10 mins
Cook Time: 0 mins
Serving Size: 4

Ingredients:
- 1 large organic zucchini, spiralized
- ¼ cup red bell pepper, diced
- ¼ cup green bell pepper, diced

Sauce Ingredients:
- 1 cup unsalted raw cashews
- 1 ½ tablespoons garlic, minced
- 2 to 3 basil leaves, fresh
- Juice of ½ lemon
- Himalayan pink salt, pinch
- ½ cup water

Instructions:
- In a large bowl, mix zucchini and peppers, set aside
- Next, add all sauce ingredients in a blender and half of the water until desired consistency.
- Pour over zucchini noodles and enjoy!

Curried Brussels Sprouts w/Sweet Potatoes

Prep time: 10 mins
Cook Time: 20 mins
Serving Size: 4

Ingredients:
- 1 ½ cup brussels sprouts, halved
- 1 small sweet potato, peeled and cubed
- 1 can (15 ounces) organic chickpeas, drained and rinsed
- 1 small yellow onion, chopped
- Vegetable broth
- ¼ teaspoon mustard seeds
- ½ teaspoon cumin
- ½ teaspoon turmeric
- 1 tablespoon garlic, minced
- ½ tablespoon ginger, minced
- ¼ teaspoon garam masala
- ½ teaspoon cilantro
- 1 can (15 ounces) coconut milk
- Sea salt and pepper (optional)
- Vegan sour cream (for topping)

Instructions:
- Heat 2 tablespoons of vegetable broth in a large pot over medium heat. Add mustard seeds and stir until they start to pop. Add onion and cook until translucent or soft.
- Add garlic, turmeric, ginger, cumin, and Marsala and stir. Next, add Sprouts, sweet potatoes, and chickpeas. Stir and coat with spices. Add coconut milk with ½ cup of broth. Reduce and simmer for 15 to 20 minutes.
- When ready to eat, add to bowl and top with vegan sour cream with cilantro. Then, enjoy!

No Squidding Calamari

Prep time: 40 mins
Cook Time: 5 mins
 Serving Size: 4

Ingredients:
- 4 to 5 large organic king oyster mushrooms
- 2 tablespoons tamari
- 1 tablespoon ground flaxseed
- 3 tablespoons water
- ½ cup unsweetened almond milk
- ½ cup all-purpose unbleached flour
- ½ cup Italian breadcrumbs (may need to grind)
- 1 teaspoon Old Bay seasoning
- 2 tablespoons dulse flakes
- 1 teaspoon onion powder
- 1 teaspoon garlic powder
- Grapeseed oil for frying
- 1 small lemon
- Parsley, for topping

Instructions:
- Clean mushrooms and remove the caps. Slice the stems into rounds. Using a small circular cookie cutter, or small knife, cut a hole in the middle of each round to make rings. Add all, except the caps, to a bowl. Then, add tamari to coat mushrooms and allow to marinate for at least 30 minutes.
- Next, make a flaxseed egg. In a small bowl, add flaxseed and water and let sit for 10 minutes. Then, add almond milk to flaxseed egg and mix.

- In a medium bowl, combine flour, breadcrumbs, old bay seasoning, dulse flakes, onion, and garlic powder and mix well.
- Drain mushrooms then add mushrooms to flaxseed/milk mixture, then add to the flour mixture to coat.
- Heat grapeseed oil to a deep skillet or fryer and heat over medium heat. Fry mushroom for 1 to 2 minutes and place them on a paper towel to drain excess oil.
- Drizzle lemon juice over cooked "calamari" and parsley.
- Enjoy!

Simply Delicious Mac-n-Cheese

Prep time: 20 min
Cook Time: 30 mins
Serving Size: 8 to 10

Ingredients:
- 4 cups of unsweetened almond milk
- 2 tablespoons garlic powder
- 2 tablespoons onion powder
- 2 tablespoons yellow mustard
- 1 tablespoon Celtic sea salt
- 1 tablespoon paprika
- ¼ teaspoon black pepper
- ¾ cup nutritional yeast
- 2 cups olive oil (cold-pressed virgin)
- 2 tablespoons of Herbamere or Spike seasoning (optional)
- 1 cup Daiya non-dairy mozzarella cheese
- 16 ounces brown rice elbow pasta (cook according to package)
- 1 tablespoon dried or fresh chopped parsley

Instructions:
- Preheat oven to 350 degrees.
- Place cooked noodles in a bowl and set aside.
- Place milk, salt, garlic and onion powders, herb seasoning, mustard, pepper, and nutritional yeast in a blender. While blending these ingredients, remove the center top from blender and pour oil in the center hole and blend until thickened.
- Pour cheese mixture over the macaroni noodles, add Daiya cheese, stir and mix well.

- Pour macaroni mixture into a large baking dish and sprinkle parsley on top for garnish. Bake for 30 to 35 minutes.

Kale with Red Bell Peppers

Prep time: 10 mins
Cook Time: 20 to 25 mins
 Serving Size: 4 to 6

Ingredients:

- 1 (16 ounce) package of fresh kale or a bunch of organic kale
- ½ medium onion, chopped
- 1 medium red bell pepper, chopped
- 1 cup organic vegetable broth
- 3 tablespoons Bragg Apple Cider Vinegar
- 1 tablespoon red pepper flakes
- 1 teaspoon vegan cane sugar

Instructions:

- In a large pot over medium heat, take a tablespoon of the vegetable broth and sauté' onions and red bell peppers until soft.
- Next, add all remaining ingredients. Bring to a boil, then simmer for 20 to 25 minutes. It's ok to add more broth if needed.

Kale and White Bean Soup

Prep time: 10 mins
Cook Time: 35 mins
Serving Size: 6

Ingredients:
- 1 bunch fresh kale, cleaned and chopped
- 1 15 ounce can cannellini beans, drained and rinsed
- 1 medium sweet potato, peeled and diced into cubes
- 1 15 ounce can diced organic diced tomatoes
- 2 each Field Roast Italian Sausage, sliced
- 1 garlic clove, minced
- ½ tablespoon onion powder
- 1 teaspoon turmeric
- ½ teaspoon thyme
- 2 containers vegetable stock
- Sea salt and pepper to taste

Instructions:
- In a large pot, heat two tablespoons vegetable stock and add garlic and sausage and sauté for 1 to 2 minutes.
- Add remaining vegetable stock, beans, tomatoes, sweet potatoes, thyme, onion powder, and turmeric.
- Bring to a simmer and cook for 20 minutes until potatoes are tender.
- Add sausage and kale and continue to cook for 15 minutes until kale is tender. Adjust seasoning to taste.

Kale Yeah It's Au Gratin w/Sweet Potato and Cauliflower

Prep time: 10 mins
Cook Time: 30 mins
Serving Size: 4

Ingredients:
- 1 bunch fresh kale, cleaned and chopped
- 1 small head cauliflower, cleaned and chopped into bite-size pieces
- 1 medium sweet potato, peeled and sliced into rounds
- 1 medium yellow onion, chopped
- 1 can coconut milk
- 1 tablespoon garlic, minced
- 2 tablespoons nutritional yeast
- 1 tablespoon rosemary
- ½ tablespoon cornstarch
- ¼ teaspoon nutmeg
- 1 teaspoon arrowroot powder
- Vegetable broth for sautéing
- Grapeseed oil to grease casserole dish

Instructions:
- Preheat oven to 350 degrees.
- Using broth, sauté onion, garlic, and kale until kale is wilted and onions are transparent. Drain and set aside.
- In a greased 9x9 casserole dish, place sweet potatoes in a single layer. Next, place bite size cauliflower pieces on top of layered potatoes. Make sure to spread evenly.
- Spread the kale mixture over the cauliflower mixture.
- In a bowl, mix together the coconut milk, nutritional yeast, arrowroot powder, cornstarch, salt, pepper,

rosemary, and nutmeg. Pour over vegetable in baking dish.

- Place in oven and bake for 25 to 30 minutes, until potatoes are cooked through. Also, the creamy sauce should be bubbling. Remove from oven and allow to cool before serving.

Vegetable Pho Soup

Prep Time: 10 mins
Cooking Time: 15 – 25 mins
Serving Size: 4

Ingredients:
- 8 cups of vegetable broth
- 2 cups of water
- 1/2 box of brown rice noodles (cook according to package)
- 1 teaspoon juice from ginger
- 2 tablespoons garlic, minced
- 2 tablespoons Bragg's aminos (soy sauce substitute)
- 3 ribs Bok Choy, sliced thin
- 1 medium white onion, sliced thin
- 1 small package Bella mushrooms, cubed or sliced
- Juice of 1 lime

Toppings (use whichever ones you like):
- Bean sprouts
- 1 small jalapeno pepper, sliced (optional)
- Sautéed extra firm tofu
- Fresh cilantro
- Fresh mint
- Fresh basil
- Green onions, diced
- Hot sauce
- Black bean garlic sauce

Instructions:
- In a large pot, add the broth, water, ginger, garlic, bok choy, onion, and mushrooms and bring to a simmer. Cover and let simmer for 15 to 25 minutes.

- Taste and add Bragg's aminos, feel free to add more aminos, if needed.
- Cook brown rice noodles according to package and make sure to drain and rinse with cold water.
- When everything is ready, add the noodles to a bowl first, then add soup and top with your favorite toppings of your choice.

Spaghetti with Cauliflower and Mushroom Sauce

Prep time: 10 mins
Cook Time: 30 mins
Serving Size: 6

Ingredients:
- 1 medium cauliflower head, cut in halves
- 1 cup baby Bella mushrooms
- ½ medium white onion, diced
- ¼ cup green bell pepper, chopped
- ¼ cup red bell pepper, chopped
- 2 garlic cloves, minced
- 1 tablespoon Italian seasoning
- ½ teaspoon turmeric
- 1 teaspoon basil
- 1 teaspoon oregano, ground
- 1 tablespoon garlic powder
- 1 tablespoon onion powder
- 1 tablespoon Black Strapped Molasses
- 2 jars (25.5 ounces) organic pasta sauce
- Sea salt and pepper, to taste
- 1 package thin spaghetti
- Vegetable broth

Instructions:
- Cook pasta according to instructions.
- Cut the cauliflower into halves and place in a food processor and pulse until they are rice-sizes pieces. Remove from processor and set aside.
- Place mushrooms in the food processor and pulse until they are rice-size pieces. Remove from processor and set aside.

- Heat 1 tablespoon of broth in a large pot over medium heat. Add onion, green bell pepper, red bell pepper, and garlic and sauté until onion is translucent.
- Add the cauliflower, mushrooms, Italian seasoning, turmeric, basil, oregano, garlic powder, and onion powder. Cook for amount 5 to 6 minutes, until the cauliflower and mushroom mixture is tender.
- Add the pasta sauce and molasses and simmer for 10 minutes. Stir occasionally.
- Lastly, add salt and pepper to taste.
- Serve over spaghetti and enjoy.

Jackfruit "No Chicken" and Dumplings

Prep time: 10 mins
Cook Time: 30 to 40 mins
Serving Size: 8

Ingredients:
- 1 can jackfruit in brine, drain and rinse
- 1 medium yellow or white onion, chopped
- 2 large carrots, cleaned and chopped
- 2 stalks celery, cleaned and chopped
- 8 cups vegetable broth
- ½ tablespoon garlic powder
- 1 teaspoon parsley
- 2 teaspoons thyme
- ½ tablespoon poultry seasoning
- Sea salt and pepper to taste
- 3 tablespoons cornstarch (optional)

Ingredients for Dumplings:
- 1 ¾ cups unbleached all-purpose flour
- 1/3 cup vegan butter, cold
- ½ teaspoon baking powder
- ¾ cup unsweetened almond milk
- ½ teaspoon salt

Instructions for Jackfruit:
- Combine jackfruit, onion, carrots, and celery in a large pot.
- Add vegetable broth. Bring to a boil, reduce heat add garlic powder, parsley, thyme, poultry seasoning, salt, and pepper and simmer covered 15 minutes or until celery and carrots are tender.
- While simmering, prepare the dumplings.

- Slowly add dumplings to the broth and simmer for an additional 15 to 20 minutes.
- In a small bowl combine cornstarch with 3 tablespoons water. Add to boiling broth. This is used to thicken the broth (optional).

Instructions for Dumplings:
- Combine flour, baking powder, salt, and cold butter with a fork until the butter is mixed in.
- Add milk a little at a time and mix until combined. You may not need to use all the milk.
- Knead a few times on a floured surface until dough is smooth. Then, use a roller to flatten the dough. Cut dough into small squares.

Bread

Zucchini Banana Nut Bread

Zucchini Banana Nut Bread

Prep time: 15 mins
Cook Time: 60 mins
Serving Size: 8 to 10 slices

Ingredients:
- 2 cups all-purpose unbleached flour
- ½ cup pure cane sugar
- ½ cup brown sugar
- 3 teaspoons baking powder
- 1 teaspoon cinnamon spice
- ¼ teaspoon nutmeg spice
- ½ teaspoon Celtic sea salt
- 1 cup shredded/diced zucchini
- 1 small mashed ripe banana
- ¼ cup unsweetened almond milk
- ¼ cup melted coconut oil
- 1 teaspoon vanilla extract
- ½ cup chopped walnuts
- 1 tablespoon flaxseed meal
- 3 tablespoons hot water
- Parchment paper

Instructions:
- Preheat oven to 350F
- In a small bowl, mix 1 tablespoon Flaxseed Meal with 3 tablespoons hot water and set aside for at least a minute. It will become gloopy. This is called a Flaxseed Egg.
- Sift flour into a mixing bowl and add the cane sugar, brown sugar, baking powder, cinnamon, nutmeg, and salt. Mix together.
- Add zucchini, mashed banana, walnuts, almond milk, coconut oil, vanilla, and flax egg to the mixing bowl and

mix. Let stand for 1 to 2 minutes. This will allow the zucchini to release more water into the mix in order to mix properly.

- Spray a 9x5 loaf pan with non-stick spray and then line it with parchment paper. Make sure the parchment hangs over the side so that when the bread is finished, you can lift out of loaf pan
- Pour batter into the parchment lined loaf pan and smooth evenly.
- Place in oven and bake for 60 minutes or until a toothpick inserted into the center comes out clean.
- Lift bread out of the loaf pan and allow to cool before slicing.

Blueberry Flax Muffins

Prep time: 15 mins
Bake Time: 25 – 30 mins
Serving Size: 1 dozen

Ingredients:
- 2 cups oat flour
- ¼ cup ground flaxseed
- 2 teaspoons baking powder
- ¼ teaspoon Celtic sea salt
- 1 teaspoon pure vanilla extract
- 4 tablespoons grapeseed oil
- 1 cup unsweetened almond milk
- 1 teaspoon apple cider vinegar
- ½ cup applesauce
- ½ cup brown sugar
- 1 ½ cup fresh blueberries

Instructions:
- Preheat oven to 375F
- In a small bowl, mix almond milk and vinegar and set aside for at least 5 minutes.
- In a large bowl, combine flour, flaxseed, baking powder, and salt. Mix well.
- Add apple sauce, oil, sugar, milk/vinegar mixture to bowl with flour. Mix until combined well. Fold in blueberries.
- Lightly grease or line a 12-tin muffin tray. Fill each halfway with muffin batter. Place in the oven until puffed, golden brown, and a toothpick inserted in the center of the muffin comes out clean.
- Allow to cool and enjoy.

Mama's "Vegan" Yeast Biscuits

Prep time: 2 ½ hours
Cook Time: 15 to 20 mins
Serving Size: 1 dozen

Ingredients:
- 1 cup unsweetened almond milk
- 1 teaspoon lemon juice
- 1 tablespoon Red Star Platinum Superior Yeast
- ¼ cup warm water
- 2 ½ cups all-purpose unbleached flour
- 1 teaspoon baking powder (aluminum free)
- ½ teaspoon baking soda
- 1 teaspoon sea salt
- 2 tablespoons pure cane sugar
- ½ cup Earth Balance vegan butter, cold

Instructions:
- In a small bowl, combine almond milk and lemon juice. Set aside.
- In another small bowl, combine the yeast and warm water. Set aside for about 5 minutes until foamy.
- In a large bowl, whisk together the flour, baking powder, baking soda, salt, and sugar. Cut in the vegan butter until pea-sized pieces are formed. Stir in the almond milk and yeast mixtures until no flour streaks remain.
- Cover with a kitchen or napkin towel and allow to rise in a warm place for 2 hours.
- Preheat oven to 400 degrees F. After the dough has risen, transfer onto a floured surface and knead for 30 seconds until dough comes together and starts to get more elastic. If too sticky, add more flour, then roll out.

- Lightly grease a cookie or line a cookie sheet with parchment paper.
- Cut dough into 12 biscuits and place onto prepared cookie sheet.
- Bake for 10- 15 minutes, until biscuits have risen and are golden brown.

Cornbread

Prep time: 10 mins
Cook Time: 25 mins
 Serving Size: 8

Ingredients:
- 1 cup yellow organic cornmeal
- 1 cup all-purpose unbleached flour
- ½ cup pure cane sugar (not granulated white sugar)
- 3 teaspoons aluminum-free baking powder
- 1 teaspoon sea salt
- 1 cup unsweetened almond milk
- 1/3 cup natural unsweetened applesauce
- 1/2 cup of melted vegan butter

Instructions:
- Preheat oven: 400 degrees
- In a bowl, combine and mix cornmeal, flour, sugar, baking powder, and salt.
- In a separate bowl, combine and mix milk, applesauce, and butter.
- Next, combine both wet and dry ingredients and mix until blended.
- Pour batter in greased pan. Bake 20-25 minutes or until golden brown.

Mama's Garlic Potato Rolls

Prep Time: 30 mins
Cook Time: 20 – 15 mins
Serving Size: 6

Ingredients:
- 1 small potato cooked and mashed
- 2 1/2 cups whole wheat pastry flour
- 2 teaspoons instant (rapid-rise) yeast
- 1 cup warm unsweetened almond milk
- 1 teaspoon sea salt
- ½ tablespoon garlic powder
- 1 ½ tablespoons maple syrup
- 1 tablespoon parsley
- 2 tablespoons vegan butter

Instructions:
- Preheat oven to 350 degrees
- In a medium bowl, combine flour, salt, and garlic powder. Set aside.
- In a separate bowl, mix yeast, milk, and maple syrup. Set aside for 5-10 minutes until a light foam appears.
- Make a hole in the center of the flour and pour the wet mixture and mashed potatoes. Mix until dough forms. Place dough on a flat surface and knead for 2 minutes.
- Divide dough into 12 rolls. Place rolls on a nonstick baking pan. Cover and leave in a warm place for an hour.
- Preheat oven to 350 degrees
- Uncover rolls and bake for 20-25 minutes until golden brown.

- After removing rolls from the oven, in a small bowl, melt the butter and add parsley, mix, and brush over rolls.

Desserts

Glazed Lemon Bundt Cake

Vegan Cinnamon Rolls

Prep time: 30 mins
Cook Time: 20 mins
Serving Size: 1 dozen

Roll Ingredients:
- 4 ½ cups unbleached all-purpose flour
- 2 tablespoons aluminum-free baking powder
- 1 teaspoon sea salt
- 2 ½ teaspoons quick-rise yeast (prepare according to package)
- 1 cup Earth Balance Vegan Butter, cut into small cubes
- 1 cup unsweetened almond milk

Filling Ingredients:
- ¼ cup Earth Balance Vegan Butter, melted
- 1 cup turbinado or brown sugar
- 1 tablespoon ground cinnamon spice

Icing Ingredients (optional):
- 1 cup organic powdered sugar
- 2 tablespoons Earth Balance Vegan Butter
- 1 teaspoon vanilla extract
- 3 teaspoons lemon juice

Instructions:
- Preheat oven 375 degrees. Line cookie sheet pan with parchment paper.

- **Rolls**: Prepare the yeast according to package directions. Set aside. Next, in a large bowl, whisk together the flour, baking powder, and salt. Add the butter cubes and use a fork or pastry cutter to cut the butter into the flour until you reach a grainy-like texture. Pour in the yeast mixture and the almond milk to make the dough.

- Using the same large bowl or a clean work surface use your hands to knead the dough together into a nice ball. Let the dough rest for 10 to 15 minutes before the next step.
- After the dough has rested, lightly flour a clean work surface and roll the dough with a rolling pin until you get a nice size rectangle.

- **Filling**: Pour the melted butter over the rectangle dough and use a pastry brush or the back of a spoon to spread evening over the dough. Next, in a small bowl mix the brown sugar and cinnamon, then sprinkle the cinnamon sugar evenly over the melted butter.

- **Let's Roll**: Starting from the longer side of the dough, use your hands to gently roll the dough up. Once rolled, use a knife to cut 12 cinnamon rolls.
- **Bake**: Place the rolls on the cookie sheet, swirl side up and bake for 20 minutes until puffed up and lightly golden. Let cool.

- **Icing**: Combine the powdered sugar, butter, vanilla extract, and lemon juice in a small bowl. Spread icing over warm cinnamon rolls. Enjoy!

Easy Like Sunday Morning Peach Cobbler

Prep time: 20 mins
Cook Time: 25 - 30 mins
Serving Size: 6 to 8

Ingredients:
- 4 to 5 fresh peaches, cleaned and sliced
- ½ cup pure cane sugar
- 2 tablespoons cornstarch
- 1 1/3 cup water
- 1 teaspoon cinnamon
- ¾ teaspoon cardamom
- ¼ teaspoon nutmeg
- 1 teaspoon vanilla extract
- 1 pie crust (I use Wholly Wholesome) cut into strips

Instructions:
- Preheat oven 350 degrees
- Combine sugar, cornstarch, water, and peaches in a saucepan.
- Over medium heat, bring to a slight boil. Stir constantly for 1 minute.
- Next, add nutmeg, cardamom, vanilla extract, and keep stirring.
- Remove from heat and pour the mixture into a casserole dish and sprinkle with cinnamon.
- Take the pie crust strips and lay across the mixture.
- Bake for 25 to 30 minutes.

Vegan Chocolate Cake

Prep Time: 15 mins
Cooking Time: 30 – 15 mins
Serving Size: 10

Ingredients for cake:
- 2 cups all-purpose unbleached flour, plus more for coating the pans
- 2/3 cup natural unsweetened cocoa powder
- 2 teaspoons baking powder
- 1 teaspoon baking soda
- 1/2 teaspoon Celtic sea salt
- 2 ounces natural unsweetened chocolate,
- 2 cups plain, unsweetened almond milk
- 2 teaspoons apple cider vinegar
- 2 sticks (8 ounces) vegan butter, plus more for coating the pans
- 1 cup packed dark brown sugar
- 2/3 cup pure cane sugar
- 1 tablespoon vanilla extract

Ingredients for frosting:
- 1 pound vegan bittersweet chocolate, finely chopped (about 3 1/4 cups)
- 4 sticks (1 pound) unsalted vegan butter, at room temperature
- 2/3 cups powdered sugar, sifted
- 1/4 teaspoon Celtic sea salt
- 1/2 cup natural unsweetened cocoa powder
- 6 tablespoons almond or rice milk
- 1 tablespoon vanilla extract

Instructions for Cake:
- Heat the oven to 350°F and arrange a rack in the middle. Coat 2 (9-inch) round cake pans generously with vegan butter. Line the bottom of each pan with a round of parchment or waxed paper, then; coat the paper with more margarine. Dust the pans all over with flour, tapping any excess out; set aside.
- Sift the measured flour, cocoa powder, baking powder, baking soda, and salt into a medium bowl; set aside.
- Using a microwave, melt the chocolate in a small bowl; set aside to cool slightly. In a medium bowl, combine the milk and vinegar; set aside.
- Using a mixer, beat the margarine and sugars on medium-high speed until fluffy and well combined. Add the melted chocolate and vanilla and beat until just combined. Scrape down the sides of the bowl. Reduce the speed to low, add a third of the flour mixture, and mix until blended well. Add a third of the milk mixture and mix until just incorporated. Continue with the remaining flour and milk mixtures, alternating between each and stopping to scrape down the sides of the bowl as needed, until all ingredients are mixed well.
- Divide the batter between the prepared pans and spread the tops evenly with a spoon or spatula. Bake until a toothpick inserted into the center comes out clean, about 30 to 35 minutes.

Instructions for Frosting:
- Using a microwave, melt the chocolate in a medium bowl; set aside to cool.
- Using a mixer, beat the butter on medium-high speed until fluffy, about 2 minutes, stopping to scrape down the sides of the bowl. Turn the mixer to low, add the sugar and salt, and mix well. Increase the speed to medium-high and beat until fluffy, about 3 minutes, stopping to scrape down the sides of the bowl.

- With the mixer on low, gradually add the cooled melted chocolate and beat until mixed well. Next, add the cocoa powder, milk, and vanilla. Beat on low until blended, and then beat on medium-high until the frosting is airy and thoroughly mixed, about 1 minute, stopping once to scrape down the sides of the bowl.

Glazed Lemon Bundt Cake

Prep Time: 20 mins
Cook Time: 45 – 50 mins
Serving Size: 10 - 12

Ingredients for Cake:

- 3 ½ cups unbleached all-purpose flour
- 2 ½ tablespoons baking powder, aluminum free
- ¼ cup cornstarch
- ¼ cup fresh squeezed lemon juice
- 3 tablespoons lemon fresh grated lemon zest
- 2 cups pure cane sugar
- 2/3 cup olive oil
- 1 2/3 cup unsweetened almond milk
- 2 tablespoons unsweetened apple sauce
- 1 teaspoon vanilla extract
- 1 teaspoon lemon extract
- ¾ teaspoon sea salt

Ingredients for Glaze:

- 3 tablespoons freshly squeezed lemon juice
- 3 tablespoons pure cane sugar

Instructions for Cake:

- Preheat oven to 350 degrees.
- In a large mixing bowl, mix flour, cornstarch, baking powder, lemon, zest, and salt.
- In a separate mixing bowl, whisk together lemon juice, sugar, oil, milk, applesauce, vanilla, and lemon extract.
- Pour wet ingredients into the bowl of dry ingredients and mix well until combined.

- Lightly oil and flour a large Bundt pan. Then, pour batter into the pan and bake for 45 – 50 minutes, or until a toothpick comes out clean.
- When ready, remove the cake from oven and allow to cool for 5 to 10 minutes before taking out of Bundt pan.

Instructions for Glaze:
- Mix lemon juice and sugar in a bowl, then, put in a small saucepan, and allow to simmer for 2 to 3 minutes.
- Use a spoon or pastry brush to brush glaze over cake.

Frosted Walnut Brownies

Prep Time: 10 mins
Cooking Time: 30 – 35 mins
Serving Size: 9

Ingredients for Brownies:
- 2 cups unbleached all-purpose flour
- 2 cups pure cane sugar
- ¾ cup unsweetened cacao or cocoa powder
- 1 teaspoon baking powder, aluminum free
- 1 teaspoon sea salt
- 1 cup water
- 1 cup olive or sunflower oil
- 1 teaspoon vanilla extract
- ¼ cup walnuts, chopped

Ingredients for Frosting:
- ½ cup cocoa powder
- 2 tablespoons agave
- ½ coconut oil, melted

Instructions for Brownies:
- Preheat oven to 350 degrees.
- In a large mixing bowl, mix flour, sugar, cocoa powder, baking powder, and salt. Next, pour in water, oil, and vanilla extract. Mix well until blended.
- Spend evenly in a 9x13 inch baking pan.
- Bake for 30 to 35 minutes. Take out of the oven and allow to cool.

Instructions for Frosting:
- Thoroughly mix all ingredients and spread over brownies. Cut into squares.

Free Bonus – 7-Day Kick Start Detox Program!

Disclaimer

It is important to note that much of this publication is based on personal experience and studies. I ask that you use this information as you see fit and at your own risk.

Nothing in this document is intended to replace common sense, legal, medical, or other professional advice, and is meant solely to inform you. Information provided in this guide, in no way substitutes your physician's advice. As always, please consult with a medical doctor before starting or conducting any health regimen.

<u>Welcome to the 7-Day Kick Start Detox Program!</u>

In today's society, it's all but quite impossible to prevent waste and toxins from accumulating inside the body. If left unattended these conditions start to impact your health and quality of life.

Daily life stressors, poor air quality, sedentary lifestyles, and poor eating habits essentially turn the body into a dump site for toxins and waste materials. Such conditions can cause you to have low energy levels, digestive problems, and can place you at risk for chronic disease.

The 7-Day Kick Start Detox Program (KDP) is designed to flush out harmful toxins and recharge the body with the nutrients it needs for optimal health. Detoxifying the body on a periodic basis can benefit everyone. To name a few of the benefits experienced are:

- Weight Loss
- Better Immune System
- Increased Energy Levels
- Radiant Skin
- Relief for abdominal issues

I am ready to assist you in this journey. However, you must be willing to commit and to understand this is not an easy journey. When you feel as though you can't make it, think about your reason for wanting a healthier lifestyle.

Much Success....Let's Go....You can do this!!

Brenda J. Bradley, PhD

7-Day Kick Start Detox Program Table of Contents

Juicing

Recently, the National Cancer Institute began a campaign to get people to do one simple thing - EAT MORE FRUITS AND VEGETABLES. Specifically, the recommendation was to eat five servings of fruit and three servings of vegetables a day. Their reasoning was simple: a diet high in fruits and vegetables will prevent or cure a wide range of ailments.

The problem, though, is that most of us don't eat enough fruits and vegetables to reap the benefits. Although the National Cancer institute recommends five servings of vegetables and three of fruits each day, the average American eats only 1-1/2 servings of vegetables and no or very little fruit on any given day.

Juicing could help solve our fruit and vegetable deficient diets.

The vegetables studied at various facilities around the country are often the same vegetables that have been juiced for years. Collard greens, kale, potatoes, mustard greens, rutabaga, peppers, carrots, and cabbage are being studied for their phytochemical content; and are the vegetables that are most commonly juiced.

Researchers are looking into the cancer-prevention capabilities of citrus fruits, grapes, and apples, the fruits most often associated with fruit juicing.

Why Juice?

Fresh juice has the ability to deliver another important group of nutrients - enzymes. Enzymes are your body's work force. Acting as catalysts in hundreds of thousands of chemical reactions that take place throughout the body, enzymes are essential for digestion and absorption of food, for conversion of digested food into body tissue, and for the production of energy at the cellular level. In fact, enzymes are critical for most of the metabolic activities taking place in your body every day.

Fruit and vegetable juices are good sources of traditional nutrients. Citrus fruits (grapefruit, oranges, etc.) provide a healthy portion of vitamin C. Carrot juice contains large quantities of vitamin A in the form of beta carotene. A number of green juices are a good source of vitamin E. Fruit juices are a good source of essential minerals like iron, copper, potassium, sodium, iodine, and magnesium, which are bound by the plant in a form that is easily assimilated during digestion.

Since juicing removes indigestible fibers, these nutrients are available to the body in much larger quantities than if the piece of fruit or vegetable was eaten whole. Because many of the nutrients are trapped in the fiber, you are only able to assimilate about 1% of the available beta carotene when you eat a raw carrot. When a carrot is juiced, removing the fiber, nearly 100% of the beta carotene can be assimilated.

Fruits and vegetables provide one more substance that is absolutely essential for good health · water. More than 65% of most of the cells in the human body are made of water, and in some tissues, like the brain, the cells can be made up of as much as 80% water. Water is absolutely essential for good health, yet most people don't consume enough water each day. Many of the fluids like coffee, tea, soft drinks, alcoholic beverages, and artificially flavored drinks contain substances that require extra water for your body to eliminate. Fruit and vegetable juices are free of these unneeded substances and are full of pure, clean water.

The National Cancer Institute's attempt to promote the health benefits for fruits and vegetables have only affected a relatively small segment of society. As more and more is written about the long-term health benefits of fruits and vegetables and as more people learn about the possibility of preventing and curing cancer, heart disease, arthritis, and a host of other diseases by making dietary changes, the fruit and vegetables trend and the popularity of juicing will continue to grow.

Let's Eat

During the next seven days you are allowed to eat! Especially, if it means the difference between you being able to finish this detox or quit because you want to eat something. No worries; however, there are some foods you are asked to avoid:

- Meat (beef, pork, turkey, chicken, etc.)
- Seafood (salmon, tilapia, trout, catfish)
- Dairy (no animal milk)
- Caffeine (coffee, caffeinated teas)
- Alcohol (scotch, beer, vodka, gin, rum, etc.)
- Carbonated beverages (sodas, seltzer water)

In addition to eliminating meat and seafood, you are asked to avoid animal by-products such as eggs, milk, and cheese. For optimal results, the recommended food choices include fresh fruit and vegetables, vegetable soups, salads, nuts and grains.

Preparation of the detox

It is best to prepare your body for a juice cleanse at least 2-3 days in advance. This means eliminating meat, caffeine, alcohol, and processed sugar. The more you can focus your diet on fruits, vegetables, and whole grains – the better your body will be prepared for the cleansing and the better the results. The day before you start, try to eat fruits and vegetables exclusively as possible. Make sure you own or have access to a juicer not a blender. You will be extracting juice not blending it.

What to expect during the detox

You may experience a shock as your body will begin to cleanse and rid itself from years of accumulated toxins. All nutrients from the juice will start pushing out toxins that have been accumulating in your body for years. As the toxins are released into the bloodstream, you many experience physical symptoms that may cause some sort of discomfort. For those who do notice any uncomfortable symptoms, this is normal! Smile, your body is releasing any bad stuff from your organs so they can function better. **I urge you to hang in there because it will get better and you will begin to feel so much better.**

Some of the symptoms you may experience as toxins are released include:

- Flu-like symptoms
- Nausea
- Rashes
- Coughing up crud
- Diarrhea or constipation
- Lack of energy
- Feeling under the weather
- Food sensitivities
- Vomiting
- Depression – our brains are very sensitive and toxins get in the tissues of our brain!
- Bad Breath
- Headaches

Usually the reactions are mild enough where you can go on with your day just fine. If stronger reactions occur, it is generally from those whose bodies have large amount of medicine or other toxins.

<u>GETTING STARTED</u>

Juicing: In order to juice, you must use a juicer, not a blender. You are going to extract the juice not blend it. It is recommended that you get a masticating juicer; they have the ability to juice leafy greens. If you are unable to find a masticating juicer, a centrifugal juicer will work. The best juicer for you will be a personal choice based on your needs and wants. Bottom line, you will be on your way to a healthier you.

How to Clean Your Vegetables and Fruit: Fill kitchen sink or boil with cold or room temperature water. Add 1/3 cup Apple Cider Vinegar and 1 tablespoon of baking soda. Allow to soak for 5 to 10 minutes, then, drain and rinsed. For vegetables such as carrots, potatoes, and celeriac that come from the ground, you may want to lightly scrub with a brush while rinsing.

Preparing Juices: Depending on your preferences, you can make your juices ahead of time or right before consuming them. All juices will last 3 days in the fridge, in an airtight mason jar. Although, some nutrients are lost, it's a slow process. Always use mason jars to store the juice and be sure to fill the jar to the top and then put the lid on. You could also prepare all your juices each morning.

Unlimited Water and Herbal Tea: During the cleansing, you can drink as much water and natural herbal tea as you like, such as, chamomile, ginger, lemon balm, peppermint, etc. Carbonated water isn't recommended because it can cause bloating.

Exercise: Limit yourself to light exercise, such as walks, yoga, and stretching. Your energy levels will change while on a juice cleanse, so pay attention to what your body needs before exercising.

> **MEDICATION: Please do not taper or stop taking prescription medications without your physician's consent.**

On Your Mark...Get Set....Let's Go!

For the next seven (7) days you will be juicing and are allowed to eat. Try to eat only one meal a day, either for lunch or dinner. Remember juicing is an easy way to consume more nutrients. And since it's from raw whole foods, your body can assimilate it completely. Enjoy the following juice recipes and feel free to make your own juice recipe. Decaffeinated herbal teas, such as lemon ginger, green tea, etc. are ok.

Start each morning with a cup of warm lemon water or room temperature water. Squeeze the juice of one-half of a lemon and add water. I usually sip a cup while getting dressed for work. If you didn't prepare the day before, this would be a good time to make some juice. I usually drink 8 to 10 ounces for breakfast, lunch, and dinner. In between breakfast, lunch, and dinner, drink water or hot herbal tea.

Here's an example of what my plan looks like:

DAYS 1 - 7

Morning:
- A cup of warm lemon water (1/2 fresh squeezed lemon & 8oz water)
- 8oz glass of prepared juice

Mid-morning: 2 hours after breakfast
- Herbal Tea

Lunch
- 8oz glass of Glorious Turmeric juice
- A small Garden Salad

Mid-day: 2 hours after lunch
- 8oz glass of Glorious Turmeric juice
- 8 -16 oz. of water
- A cup of herbal tea

Dinner
- 8oz glass of Pineapple Cucumber Beet Juice

Evening Snack: 2 hours after dinner
- Water or Tea

Juice Recipes

The following juice recipes are quick and easy! **Put ingredients in a juicer (not blender) and ENJOY!** You may need to add more that what the recipe calls for—and that's okay!

Glorious Turmeric	Sunset Passion
Apples - 2 medium	Apples (golden delicious) - 2 medium
Carrots - 3 medium	Beet Roots - 2 beet
Celery - 3 large stalks	Carrot - 1 large
Ginger Root - 1 thumb	Orange (optional) - 1 fruit
Lemon – 1 lemon (peeled)	Pepper (sweet red) - 1 medium
Pears - 2 medium	Sweet Potato - 1 sweet potato.
Turmeric Root - 6 thumb	

Green Beauty	Ginger Beet
Apples - 2 medium	Orange - 1 medium
Celery - 4 stalk, large	Kale leaves
Cucumber - 1 cucumber	Green apple - 1 medium
Ginger Root - 1 thumb	Carrot-1 large
Kale - 6 leaf	Beet, 1 large
Lemon - 1/2 fruit	Ginger - 1-inch piece of peeled fresh

Rooty-Tooty	Pineapple Refresher
Celeriac Root– 1 medium	Beet– 1 medium
Apples – 2 medium	Apple – 1 medium
Carrots – 3 large	Cucumber– 3 large
Ginger Root – 1 thumb	Pineapple – 1 cup

The Beet Goes On	Heart Beet
Beet Root - 1 beet	Apple - 1 medium
Cabbage (red) - 2 leaf	Beet Root - 1 beet
Carrots - 3 medium	Carrots - 12 medium
Lemon - 1/2 fruit	Lemon - 1/2 fruit
Orange - 1 fruit	Oranges (peeled) - 2 each
Pineapple - 1/4 fruit	
Spinach - 2 handfuls	

Kidney Delight	Carrot-Ginger Calmer
1 Sprig Fresh Parsley Leaves and Stems	Carrots – 2 carrots
½ Bunch fresh Dandelion leaves	Celery – 1 celery stalk
1 whole organic cucumber or ½ celery stalk	Potato – 1 potato medium
2 Limes	Ginger-root – 1 Thumb
Ginger Root – 1 Thumb	
Turmeric - 1 tsp powder	

Make It Green	Kale Yeah
Apples - 2 medium	Apple - 1 medium
Celery - 3 stalk, large	Bell Pepper (red) - 1 medium
Cucumber - 1 cucumber	Carrots - 3 medium
Ginger Root - 1/2 thumb	Cilantro - 1 handful
Lemon - 1/2 fruit	Collard Greens - 1 cup
Lime - 1 fruit	Kale - 4 leaf
Parsley - 1 bunch	
Spinach - 2 cups	

True Green	Wonderful Ginger Ale
Granny Smith Apples - 2 medium	Apples - 3 medium
Green Bell Pepper - 1 medium	Celery - 2 stalk, large
Carrots - 3 medium	Cucumber - 1 cucumber
Cucumber - 1 medium	Ginger Root - 1 thumb
Spinach - 2 cup	Lime - 1 fruit
Tomato - 1 medium whole	

Green Lemonade	Incredible Hulk
Apples - 2 medium	Apples - 2 medium
Cucumber - 1 cucumber	Cucumber – 1 medium
Kale - 4 leaf	Celery - 3 stalk, large
Lemon - 1 fruit	Grapes - 15 grapes
Spinach - 2 cups	Lime - 1 fruit
	Spinach - handful

The Roots	Call Me Pretty Red
Beet Root - 1 medium	Apples - 2 medium
Sweet Potato – 1 medium	Beet Root - 1 beet
Carrots - 10 medium	Carrots - 4 medium
	Cucumber - 1/2 cucumber
	Dandelion Greens or Spinach- 1 cup, chopped
	Ginger Root - 1 thumb
	Kale (optional) - 2 leaf
	Orange (peeled) - 1 fruit

Orange Delight	Detoxifier
Apples - 2 medium	Beets – 2 medium
Celery - 3 stalk, large	Carrots – 5 large
Orange (peeled) - 1 fruit	Ginger Root - 1/4 thumb
Pears - 2 medium	Lemon - 1/2 fruit
Sweet Potato - 1 sweet potato	Apples – 2 medium

Salad and Soup Recipes

Simple House Salad

Ingredients
- Romaine lettuce - 1 cup chopped
- Cherry tomatoes – ½ cup sliced in halves
- Cucumbers – ¼ cup chopped
- Red Onion – 1 slice chopped
- Vinaigrette salad dressing

Place ingredients in a medium bowl and toss with vinaigrette. Serve immediately unless you're taking salad to work, keep dressing separate.

Spinach Salad

Ingredients
- A handful baby spinach
- Strawberries – ½ cup sliced
- Carrots - 1/2 cup shredded
- Cucumbers – 1/4 chopped
- Vinaigrette salad dressing

Place ingredients in a medium bowl and toss with vinaigrette. Serve immediately unless you're taking salad to work, keep dressing separate.

Kale Salad

Ingredients
- Kale – 1 cup chopped
- Sunflower seeds – ¼ cup
- Red Cabbage – ½ cup shredded
- Carrots – ½ cup shredded
- Lemon Vinaigrette dressing

Place ingredients in a medium bowl and toss with vinaigrette. Can be made ahead of time and stored in refrigerator for up to 24 hours.

Broccoli Salad

Ingredients
- Broccoli Crowns – 2 large chopped
- Cherry tomatoes – 1½ cup sliced in halves
- Red Onions – ¼ cup chopped
- Dried Raisins or Cranberries – ¼ cup
- Walnuts – ½ cup chopped

Dressing
- Raw Cashews (unsalted) ¾ cup soaked
- Water – ¼ cup
- Agave – 1 tablespoon
- Garlic – ½ teaspoon minced
- Celtic Sea Salt – ½ tsp

1. Place cashews in a bowl and soak for 2 to 3 hours or overnight. Drain cashews. Add to blender with the rest of the dressing ingredients. Blend until smooth and creamy.
2. Place salad ingredients in a medium bowl and toss with dressing. Serve immediately or later when chilled.

No Lettuce Salad

Ingredients
- Orange Bell Pepper – 1 cup chopped small
- Yellow Bell Pepper – 1 cup chopped small
- Radishes – about 5 each sliced thin
- Broccoli Crown – 2 cups chopped small
- Cucumber – 1 small to medium chopped small
- Red seedless grapes – 1 cup halves
- Fresh Parsley – 2 tablespoons chopped

Dressing
- Garlic clove, minced
- Red wine vinegar – 2 tablespoons
- Apple cider vinegar – 1 tablespoon
- Lemon Juice– 1 tsp
- Dijon mustard – 1 tablespoon

3. Mix all dressing ingredients together and set aside.
4. Combine all salad ingredients; pour dressing over salad and mix well.
5. Cover and store in refrigerator for an hour or two.

Garden Vegetable Soup

Ingredients
- Vegetable broth - 3 tablespoons
- Yellow onion - 1 1/2 cups, chopped
- Carrots - 2 cups, chopped
- Celery -1 1/4 cups chopped
- Garlic - 4 cloves, minced
- Vegetable Broth - 4 cups
- Diced Tomatoes -2 (14.5 oz.) cans (undrained)
- Potatoes 3 cups peeled and 1/2-inch thick chopped
- Green Beans - 1 1/2 cups chopped frozen or fresh
- Corn - 1 1/4 cups frozen or fresh (optional)
- Peas - 1 cup frozen or fresh
- Fresh Parsley - 1/3 cup chopped
- 2 bay leaves
- 1/2 tsp dried thyme
- Salt and freshly ground black pepper

Instructions

1. Heat 3 to 4 tablespoons vegetable broth in large pot over medium heat.

2. Add onions, carrots, and celery and sauté 4 minutes then add garlic and sauté 30 seconds longer. You may need to add more broth. Make sure broth doesn't dissolve.

3. Add in 4 cups broth, tomatoes, potatoes, parsley, bay leaves, thyme and season with salt and pepper to taste (for more flavor add in more dried herbs as desired).

4. Bring to a boil, and then add green beans.

5. Reduce heat to medium-low, cover and simmer until potatoes are tender, about 20 - 30 minutes, then add corn and peas and cook 5 minutes longer.

6. Serve warm and enjoy!

Brown Rice Veggie Soup with Chickpeas

Ingredients
- Vegetable broth - 5 cups
- Brown Rice - ½ cup cooked
- Chickpeas, 1 (15 oz.) can drained, and rinsed
- Carrot -1 medium, sliced or chopped
- Broccoli - 1 cup chopped
- Spinach - 1 cup
- Tomatoes - 1 (15 oz.) can chopped or diced
- 2 teaspoons dried basil
- 1 teaspoon dried oregano
- Salt and pepper to taste

Instructions

Add broth to large saucepan and bring to boil. Add chickpeas, carrots, broccoli, tomatoes, basil, and oregano and simmer for 20 to 25 minutes.

Next, add the cooked brown rice and baby spinach. Reduce the heat to low, cover and simmer for 5 to 10 minutes. Add salt and pepper to taste (optional)

Enjoy!

129

CONGRATULATIONS

Change is inevitable!

I want to take this time to congratulate you on taking this amazing journey in an effort to take control of your health. The main reason for the 7 Day Kick Start Detox Program is to educate and show you ways to eat healthier and to feel good about the choices you make. You now have the tools needed to help you change your life for the better.

I am so proud of you and you should be especially proud as well. Now that you have experienced this journey, be sure to share your positive testimony with others and help them to take control of their health as well.

In closing, I would like to leave you with one of my favorite bible verses:

And be not conformed to this world; but be ye transformed by the renewing of your mind, that ye may prove what is that good and acceptable and perfect Will of God
(Romans 12:2)

Here's to good health,

Brenda J. Bradley, PhD

Contact Brenda T. Bradley, PhD

Phone: 1-(888)-567-2822

Email: Brenda@drbtbradley.com

Website: www.drbtbradley.com

Twitter: www.twitter.com/drbrendabradley

Instagram: www.instagram.com/docbrad67

9 781947 445673